Women
of the Revolution

BRAVERY AND SACRIFICE ON THE SOUTHERN BATTLEFIELDS

ROBERT M. DUNKERLY

Charleston London
THE
History
PRESS

Published by The History Press
Charleston, SC 29403
www.historypress.net

Cover image: Photo illustration by Marshall Hudson featuring reenactment of the British Camp at Eutaw Springs, South Carolina.

First published 2007
Second printing 2010

Manufactured in the United States

ISBN 978.1.59629.389.2
Library of Congress Cataloging-in-Publication Data
Dunkerly, Robert M.
Women of the Revolution : bravery and sacrifice on the Southern fields /
Robert M. Dunkerly.
p. cm.
Includes bibliographical references.
ISBN-13: 978-1-59629-389-2 (alk. paper)
1. Southern States--History--Revolution, 1775-1783--Women. 2. United
States--History--Revolution, 1775-1783--Women. 3. Women--Southern
States--History--18th century. 4. Women--Southern States--Biography. 5.
Southern States--History--Revolution, 1775-1783--Social aspects. 6. United
States--History--Revolution, 1775-1783--Social aspects. 7. Southern
States--History--Revolution, 1775-1783--Campaigns. 8. United
States--History--Revolution, 1775-1783--Campaigns. I. Title.
E276.D86 2007
973.3082--dc22
2007040045

Contents

Acknowledgements   7

Introduction   9

Part I. Setting Time and Place   11
The Values of the Eighteenth-century World   13
The Eighteenth-century Woman   27

Part II. Early Battles   37
Moores Creek, North Carolina   39
Savannah, Georgia   49

Part III. Spring and Summer 1780   51
Charleston, South Carolina   53
Brattonsville, South Carolina
    (Williamson's Plantation)   57
Hanging Rock, South Carolina   63
Camden, South Carolina   67
Fishing Creek, South Carolina   71
Stallions, South Carolina   73
Part IV. Fall 1780   77

Contents

Kings Mountain, South Carolina   79

Part V. Winter 1780–81   87
Cowpens, South Carolina   89
Guilford Courthouse, North Carolina   93

Part VI. Spring and Summer 1781   101
Fort Motte, South Carolina   103
Ninety Six, South Carolina   109
Alston House, North Carolina
    (House in the Horseshoe)   115
Eutaw Springs, South Carolina   121
Lindley's Mill, North Carolina   125
Southeastern North Carolina   127
Bacon's Bridge, South Carolina   131

Conclusion   133
Preserving the Past   135
Notes   143
Bibliography   151
About the Author   157

Acknowledgements

S everal people helped with this project. I would like to thank Mickey Crowell of the Kings Mountain Historical Museum; Virginia Fowler of Cowpens National Battlefield; Nancy Stewart of Guilford Courthouse National Military Park; Hattie L. Squires of Moores Creek National Military Park; Brian Robeson and Frank Stovall of Musgrove Mill State Historic Site; historians John Rees and Don Hagist; Loyalist expert Todd Braisted; researchers Deb Peterson, Elizabeth Melton, Arlene Mackey and Elaine Sprinkle; and Jon Zachman of the Greensboro Historical Museum. John Robertson provided the excellent maps. Researcher Karen A. Smith assisted by graciously sharing her cutting edge work on women's clothing from primary sources. Her final product will be a valuable contribution to colonial scholarship.

Introduction

The women of the Revolution and their deeds are too numerous to recount in any single book. Women were active on both sides, in every area and in nearly every military action. No single book could cover all of the activities of those who were actively involved.

This work takes a different approach to the topic of women in the Revolution. There are nearly a dozen existing titles about this topic, ranging from general overviews of women to others highlighting famous women to those that emphasize their contributions as founding mothers. There are also more detailed studies about women in the conflict: analyzing the camp followers, the spies, the soldiers like Deborah Sampson; works that examine women's roles, their changing political rights and the conflict's effect on them.

This study does not intend to study the role of women or their larger contributions, nor does it romanticize them or retell inspiring stories of women who faced invaders on their doorsteps. Like the men they served with, some women rose to the occasion and helped their cause and others acted with less than grace, but all were deeply affected by events and caught up in the struggle. Unfortunately, many of the stories were only passed down orally until recorded one hundred years later by historians. These accounts were often one-sided, exaggerated and embellished.

What this work hopes to cover is the presence of women on specific battlefields, no matter what their part. Some were active participants, others mere observers. From researching the records, one thing is clear: women were there, at nearly every fight, yet they are invisible to us today. Military records speak only of the men. Historians in the nineteenth and twentieth centuries relied on those records to write their studies and interpretations of the battles. Women may have been mentioned, but they often were not. The records were produced by, and written about, men. Most of the women who were present at these events were probably illiterate, and few left accounts of their experiences.[1]

Until the 1960s, most histories of the Revolution focused on military and political events. New ground was broken in that decade as historians began to examine the roles of women and other minorities, but their studies were often focused on upper-class women, or they studied women's roles in the political realms. Women who followed the armies or were present on battlefields received little attention. Several good studies were done in the 1980s and 1990s on camp followers, but few have examined women at specific battle sites of the Carolinas.

Women were involved in nearly every battle of the war. They were camp followers, performing vital functions that kept the armies running. They were civilians, caught up in the movements of armies. They were spies and scouts, using their freedom of movement to their advantage. They often came to the battlefields to help nurse the wounded. Sometimes they fought as well, either openly as women or disguised as men.

Unlike warfare among the large armies of North and South in the Civil War, during the Revolution women were commonly attached to or involved with the eighteenth-century armies and their campaigns. The nature of the war in the Southern colonies often put civilians into the fray; this was a war among militias, among neighbors.

There is an important distinction to draw, and it will be more fully explored below. Some women were attached to the armies; others were accompanying the militia or caught up in the guerilla warfare that raged among civilians. The experiences of these two types of women differed greatly.

Thus in the case of militia (Loyalist or Whig), women were often in or near battles, and encountered armies and the small foraging or raiding parties that roamed the countryside. Women frequently visited husbands, brothers and sons in militia camps. They often were with the armies as refugees. They were in the front lines, since in this guerilla war the front line was everywhere.

Those who were attached to regular British and American armies shared experiences that were similar to those who fought in the large Northern battles. These ladies were part of the army and subject to its military discipline. They marched, received rations, suffered from the elements, were subject to military discipline and sometimes found themselves in combat.

All of the women who were involved in these battles played important, if little-known, roles. Their stories have largely not been recognized. This work attempts to bring them to the forefront.

Part I
Setting Time and Place

The Values of the
Eighteenth-century World

The scene was repeated time and time again on battlefields: as the smoke clears and the firing ceases, soldiers move out across a battlefield littered with dead and wounded. Dismounted cannons, abandoned wagons, dead horses and the debris of battle: broken muskets, abandoned packs and overturned fences litter the area. Amid the exhausted soldiers, here and there, are women. They are part of the army, and they have experienced the battle as well.

Before going into detail about the women and their battlefields, we must first understand them and their world. During the Revolution, large areas of Georgia and the Carolinas were divided in sentiment. The fighting that erupted here was brutal and bitter. While Continental and British units were active in the region, much of the fighting was done by rival American and Loyalist militias. Women were actively involved in this fighting, and in support roles: spying, making ammunition and working for the armies.

Warfare, especially that which erupted across the Carolinas and Georgia, formed an environment where social norms broke down. Removed from the constraints of "normal" society, women were able to move into more nontraditional arenas. In an emergency situation, women were accepted in ways and in places that they may normally not have been. Yet while gender roles may have blurred, they did not break. Gender roles were clearly defined in this society that placed an emphasis on standing and class.[2]

The traditional female realm was "housekeeping," as the term they used, meaning child care, food preparation and making clothing, as well as tending crops, running the store, raising the animals and whatever other chores existed. When a woman moved outside of this sphere, both women and men generally considered it a temporary situation. Her normal realm was domestic space.[3]

Misconceptions surround the legal rights of women in colonial America. Single women or widows enjoyed many privileges such as making contracts, bringing lawsuits and managing estates. Many a widow ran her husband's business or farm as an independent businessperson.

A female who married, however, immediately found her rights superseded by those of her husband. These women lost their legal voice, as once joined to a husband, the woman's independent status was absorbed by him. Of course, situations varied widely by colony, local region and individual circumstances. Some married women could achieve a measure of legal autonomy, though the means by which and ease of which they did so varied.[4]

In the eighteenth century, women were considered weaker, less moral and possessing less capacity for reason, control and logic. Women were thought to be devious, and their presence in a male arena like a military camp could be threatening or destabilizing. Women were tolerated, but only in traditional or socially accepted women's roles.[5]

Women were expected by society to be moral, which meant married and domestically employed. Thus the armies who accepted women had them perform support roles, like nursing and laundry. These were the two most important assignments for women with the armies, laundry being the most common.[6]

That said, women often did temporarily assume men's roles while husbands were away. Women adapted to circumstances in a situation that interrupted normalcy, such as war. While women were expected to be moral and stay within socially acceptable realms, eighteenth-century society was not as caught up in morality and sensibility as its Victorian descendants would be. Gender roles could blur when occasion demanded, and many women living in frontier areas of the colonies were caught up in circumstances where normal law, order and society had broken down. Often women were caught in situations that demanded that they pick up weapons and fight, or take on other nontraditional roles.[7]

The wives, daughters, sisters and girlfriends of soldiers were as actively involved in the conflict as males were. How did women feel about the conflict? As with the common Revolutionary soldiers, we have some leads, but often are left with only conjecture. That many women wholeheartedly supported the cause (be it British or American) is beyond a doubt. They struggled, faced hardships and made sacrifices often equal to the soldiers they accompanied.[8]

Nearly all women knew how to spin; it was an essential skill for females. *Photo by Britney Robinson.*

No doubt a bond formed among women who were a minority in a very male environment, like a military camp or battlefield. Certainly women were segregated (both by choice and by circumstance) based on the same principles that segregated men: race, social class, language, common background, education, etc. Most of the women we will encounter at the battlefields discussed below were of the lower, or common, sort.[9]

In certain areas of camps or forts, when away from the men, women had a level of privacy (at the camp kitchens or while mending clothing, for example). Here they could form bonds of assistance and friendship and interact with each other. Networks could form only in seclusion, as much of their time was not their own, and their tasks kept them busy.[10]

For most camp followers attached to the armies, or women visiting militia camps, there simply was no privacy. Often they might be the only female, or one of the few, amid a large group of soldiers, wagon drivers, officers and other men. In such cases, they would have had to make the best of their situation.

Women attached themselves to the armies, and the armies had to deal with their refusal to stay behind. British forces often regulated how many women could accompany each regiment or company. The vast majority were wives or girlfriends of soldiers. If accepted and allowed to accompany the unit (in garrison or in the field), they were "on the strength" of the regiment; in other words, they were official members of the unit, with all the benefits and requirements that this entailed.[11]

Not only did women force their presence onto the armies, but historian Holly Mayer also argues that "camp followers were necessary to the survival of the military." They performed support services and functions for armies that did not have large infrastructures or logistical support services. Unlike the armies of the Civil War, the forces that fought in the Revolution did not have well-developed medical, supply and other logistical services, and those that existed often broke down or were severely stressed.[12]

Many historians have argued that armies are a reflection of the societies they come from. If this is the case, what do the British and American armies of 1775–83 tell us about those late eighteenth-century societies?[13]

European armies of the 1600s and 1700s always included women, in various capacities. The forces of the American War of Independence built on and used those earlier models; they were ingrained. While British authorities may not have liked it, women had accompanied its armies for centuries, and the trend continued at the start of the American war.[14]

Mending clothing in camp, a never-ending chore. *Photo by author.*

On the Continental side, the Americans initially hoped to form an army that reflected its democratic principles. The Revolutionaries desired an army of citizens, not a standing, full-time, professional army. They viewed the professional armies of Germany, France and England with mistrust. Citizens volunteered to serve "with the military, not in it," as historian Holly Mayer asserts.[15]

Thus for a variety of reasons—including social views that affected the formation of armies, the desires of women to contribute to the cause, the desires of husbands and wives to stay together and the needs that women fulfilled for the armies—women in the late eighteenth century were attached to armies in ways that we do not see with the later armies of the American Civil War.

The research of historian John U. Rees illustrates that women, especially in the American army, served a vital role by performing "practical tasks" like washing and sewing. This was often done for the small group in which a woman's husband or boyfriend belonged. The importance of these support services increased as the war went on and the American army's infrastructure wore down. The Continental army had difficulty through the entire conflict with its supply and transportation system, which only worsened as the war progressed. The women were tolerated, and permitted to be present, since they served a useful purpose.[16]

In examining how and under what circumstances females were with the armies, we find a variety of situations. Women "on the strength" in a British unit received half rations, were paid sixpence per day and had other privileges. They were also subject to military discipline and followed the rules and regulations of the army. Women serving with the American army could also receive rations and were considered part of the unit, but were also under martial law like any soldier with the army. Many of these ladies were wives of soldiers; often they were refugees with nowhere else to go.[17]

This could present a problem to an army if the women were not managed carefully. The British had developed a series of policies by this point in time that regulated the presence of women. A soldier had to have his officer's permission to marry, and the officer was to ensure that the woman was of good moral character and industrious.[18]

Regulations stated that an officer had to make a "strict inquiry...into the morals of the Woman." He was to determine "whether she is sufficiently known to be industrious, and able to earn her bread." Wives of soldiers were expected to be "honest, laborious Women." While women were tolerated, commanders often considered them a drain on resources.[19]

Examples abound in the Northern campaigns. In 1776 and 1777, British General William Howe allowed six women per company with his forces in the field as they campaigned across New York, New Jersey and Pennsylvania. His fellow officer, General John Burgoyne, allowed three per company in his campaign of 1777 that ended in Saratoga. These women were fed, clothed and supplied from the army's military stores. While in the field, they served as nurses after battles such as Brandywine, Germantown and Saratoga.[20]

The army's women were also subject to military discipline like the soldiers. In June of 1778, British General Henry Clinton ordered that "the Women of the Army are constantly to march upon the flanks of the Baggage of their respective Corps, the Provost Martial has received positive Orders to Drum out any Woman who shall dare to disobey this Order." Other punishments included the stocks and pillory, whipping, loss of rations and even death.[21]

Females with the army shared in its fate, good or bad. These camp followers suffered from lack of adequate clothing and poor food, and they often lived outside without shelter when on the march. They shared the sufferings and deprivations of the soldiers they accompanied.[22]

These women illustrate the variety of clothing worn in the Carolina backcountry. On the left the woman is wearing a bed jacket, kerchief and petticoat; the one on the right is wearing a gown. *Photo by Karen A. Smith.*

Revolutionary War combat was fought at close quarters, and often cold steel came into play. Swords, bayonets, knives and tomahawks inflicted terrible wounds on the body. Women, especially those in a camp or among wagons in the rear, were often caught in brutal close quarters fighting when they did find themselves caught up in a battle.

Officers referred to women who were with the army as "baggage"— they were seen as belonging with the horses, wagons, ambulances and other support services. They provided critical support to armies that did not have large logistical support services. Therein lies the key to their acceptance, or tolerance.[23]

Thus women were accepted by the army, though regulated to serve in domestic capacities. While in garrison they often cooked (men did this in messes while in the field). Women could also perform odd jobs like sewing, selling supplies or herding sheep and cattle. Some women earned their keep as servants for officers. Many others were washerwomen. Army officers set rates for laundry and oversaw the businesses as they did for any other civilian contractor or supplier.[24]

Women, unlike soldiers, were ineligible for pensions or other benefits. A woman whose husband was killed found herself alone and often without means of support. Official military policy was to return widows and orphans home, but often they managed to stay with the armies, as it was a means of support.[25]

The subject of women in the Revolution and camp followers naturally brings thoughts of prostitutes and women of ill repute who followed the armies. While many such women did attach themselves to garrisons and armies in the field, the majority of women who accompanied soldiers were those described above: wives or servants, who often had approval to be present and served an important function. Historian Linda Grant DePauw wrote that, "Far from being harlots or women of vicious character, army women tended to be the most respectable and best behaved of army wives."[26]

The prostitutes who earned their living from the armies were a hardy lot, for it was a dangerous trade. Often alone and obviously vulnerable, these women lived in fear of robbery, murder, rape and abuse, as they operated in an illegal and socially unacceptable realm.

One colonel who patrolled the American camps at New York City recorded his experiences with prostitutes who worked at a field owned by St. Paul's Church, known as "Holy Ground." He wrote, "At first I thought nothing could exceed them for Impudence and Immodesty, but I found the more I was acquainted with them the more they excelled in their Brutality. To mention the Particulars of their Behavior would so pollute the Paper I write upon that I must excuse myself."[27] Living in a lawless and dangerous world, these women adapted to their surroundings. While already mentally and physically strong, their existence in dangerous environments made them more so.

Records from South Carolina indicate that private Ezekiel Adams of the Sixth South Carolina Regiment was charged with "abuseing his wife" in June of 1779. In his defense, he maintained "he was only playing with her." For his actions he received thirty-five lashes. Thus, women could sometimes be protected by the army and its laws, but not always.[28]

Women serving with the militia (whether Loyalist or Whig) had a different experience than those with the British and American regular armies. Militia service put families into warfare, as sons, brothers, fathers and uncles often served together. It was not uncommon for women to visit militia camps. They often delivered supplies or provided intelligence, especially when sons and husbands were in local units. Often women were with militia groups that were ambushed, or were attached to militia units in the field.[29]

While a handful of women did serve in the ranks by disguising themselves as males, it was rare. Such action was absolutely discouraged, and women were punished if discovered. It went against social norms of the period, and while women did manage to move into nontraditional roles, this was one action that was not socially acceptable. Only two documented cases are known of this on the American side, and no women are known to have fought as males for the British.[30]

In the Northern battles, many women accompanied the large British and American armies. They were present in garrisons and camps, and often accompanied the armies into the field during campaigns. In one battle a Connecticut soldier witnessed women "exposing themselves where the shots were flying, to strip the dead." He stated, "I saw one woman while thus employed struck by a cannon ball and literally dashed to pieces."[31]

During the savage battle of Brandywine, Pennsylvania, in September, 1777, the women of the Sixth Pennsylvania Regiment, who were "frequently cautioned as to the danger of coming into the line of fire," took "empty canteens of their husbands and friends and returned with them filled with water" during the "hottest part of the engagement." Women even made it into the trenches to serve food and perform other duties during the siege of Yorktown, Virginia, in 1781.[32]

General Washington grudgingly accepted women in his army, though he did not like it, calling them "a clog upon every movement." Throughout the war, Washington gave many instructions regarding the issuing of rations to women, where and how they were to march with the troops and other management concerns.[33]

The presence of these women forced commanders and leaders to attend to their needs and manage their participation. Joseph Reed, governor of Pennsylvania, recommended that the state assembly fund not only new clothing for the Pennsylvania regiments, but also a "new gown, silk handkerchief, and a pair of shoes" for the women with them.[34]

Women played critical, if little-known, roles in many of the significant battles of the Southern theater. Mary Patton of the Tennessee frontier made the gunpowder used by the American forces at Kings Mountain; Kate Fowler got critical news to the British garrison at Ninety Six that changed the course of the siege; the night before the battle of Cowpens, Kate Barry helped round up local militia and in the aftermath Mrs. Goudelock may have inadvertently saved Lieutenant Colonel Banastre Tarleton from capture; Rebecca Motte broke the indecisive siege of Fort Motte; Sarah Featherstone helped ensure a British victory at Fishing Creek.

Sewing in camp.
Photo by author.

The war divided couples as it divided communities. Mercy Bedford, of Rutherford County, North Carolina, sided with the Whigs. Her husband Jonas was a Loyalist, and fought with the British at Kings Mountain, where he was captured. Despite Mercy's support of the cause, American troops raided her farm for supplies. At various times she supplied provisions for the American troops in the area. After the war, the North Carolina General Assembly restored the property to her, as Jonas had fled to England.[35]

Most of what we know of the women on these Southern battlefields comes to us from two main sources: contemporaries who discussed them in reports, pension statements and letters, and sources more removed from the events and participants, such as family lore and local history that was passed down orally until the late nineteenth century.

The writings of various officers like Lieutenant Colonel Henry Lee, General Nathanael Greene, Lord Charles Cornwallis, Lieutenant Colonel Banastre Tarleton and others mention women in the camps and on the battlefields. Their presence is also discussed in the letters of private soldiers, and in their pension statements. The observations of these eyewitnesses are often the most reliable, and least detailed, of the sources.

Unfortunately, most of the women themselves did not (or could not) write about their experiences. They may have told their stories to friends and neighbors and they may have been local celebrities, but often their true stories were lost as that generation passed on, and later descendants romanticized and distorted, intentionally and unintentionally, what had been passed down. Much of what we know of them has been shrouded in mystery and myth.

Not only are they not given full justice in written records—often only mentioned in passing—but women are sometimes even left nameless. This is often the case when a husband was an officer or local leader, and the wife is simply referred to as Mrs. Jones, for example. Every effort has been made to name each individual in the sections that follow.

Many of these stories were collected between the 1840s and 1880s by historians like Daniel Stinson of Chester County, South Carolina, who knew many of the Revolutionary War veterans; Eli Caruthers of Guilford County, North Carolina; Maurice Moore of York County, South Carolina; J.B.O. Landrum of Spartanburg, South Carolina; Elizabeth Ellet of New York, who collected research for her books on women in the Revolution; writer Benson Lossing of Connecticut; and historian Lyman C. Draper of Wisconsin.

By the time these stories were collected, they had been handed down for various periods of time, in some cases one generation to another, in other instances up to one hundred years. Clouded memories and a desire to immortalize one's ancestors undoubtedly led to one-sided and often incomplete stories.

Thus, in many ways, this work is an analysis of the information as much as it is a history of the women: the story of the stories. It is important to see where the accounts came from and learn how they were recorded, altered and modified. To get at the true people of the past, we must attempt to remove, or at least be aware of, the filter through which writers of the past recorded and judged them.

This part of the work was not intentional at first, but became more important as research and analysis progressed. In many cases, it is nearly impossible to know the women of the past: details are too sketchy, stories are too romanticized and in some cases even their names were not considered worth noting by previous historians. Thus it became imperative to reconstruct as many details of each event as possible, and analyze the sources of each story.

One last word about terminology. As stories from the Revolution were recorded and passed on, writers referred to the Americans as "Patriots." Claiming victory, they could also claim the virtuous side. "Whig" was another term for the Americans, or Rebels, as this was a political party that favored rights for the colonists. Loyal colonists who sided with the British were derogatorily referred to as "Tories." In this work, I use the terms "American" and "Whig" along with "Loyalist."

Regardless of their role in the conflict or the side they supported, the conflict affected all women who experienced it. For many it involved suffering, hardship and financial loss. Betsy Ambler Brent wrote two decades later,

> *The only possible good from the entire change in our circumstances was that we were made acquainted with the manners and situation of our own Country, which we otherwise should never have known; added to this, necessity taught us to use exertions which our girls of the present day know nothing of, We Were forced to industry to appear genteelly, to study Manners to supply the place of Education, and to endeavor by amiable and agreeable conduct to make amends for the loss of fortune.*[36]

The Eighteenth-century Woman

Now that we know the world they inhabited, we must attempt to get to know the women who accompanied the army onto a battlefield. We do not know much about the particular women in the specific examples that follow this chapter, but in looking at women's skills in general, we may get a feel for the type of abilities and knowledge that they had. This helps us somewhat to round out the often dry and usually limited facts that appear in records that mention women.

Limited statistics indicate that the average height of a colonial woman was about five feet, two inches. There was a range of about twelve inches between taller and shorter. Europeans seem generally to have been an inch or two shorter than Americans.[37]

Most working-class women had skills such as animal husbandry, gardening, cooking, weaving and spinning. The last task was considered an essential female skill, and was nearly universally taught to young women.

Most women knew something of weeding fields, planting, harvesting, raising animals, tending livestock, shearing sheep and milking cattle and goats. Typical farm chores also included putting up vegetables and fruit, preserving meat, helping in the fields, tending the poultry and fetching water. Some of these skills would have been useful in the field with an army.[38]

Women wore a variety of clothing in the eighteenth century. Then, as with modern fashion, there was no generic "colonial" clothing. Season, ethnicity, class, available materials and personal preference all played into what women wore. The undergarment worn directly against the body was the shift, which extended to mid-calf or knee length. Shifts were most commonly made of linen, some locally grown, some imported from Ireland.

Most women were skilled in gardening, tending crops and raising animals. *Photo by Brittney Robinson.*

Stays were support garments generally made with whalebone or baleen (whale cartilage). A woman wore her stays over her shift and under her gown. Stays provided posture, supported the back and actually made it easier to lift while doing common camp work. Karen A. Smith's research indicates that stays were not uncommon among women of all social classes.[39]

Over the shift and stays, a woman had many choices in her apparel. Recent research by Smith reveals that in the South, gowns, defined as full-length dresses, were the most commonly referenced item in extant wills and estate inventories for the South Carolina backcountry. A garment found in the mid-Atlantic, and one that would have traveled south with settlers traveling down the Great Wagon Road and with those coming with the armies, was the short gown, a sleeved, upper body garment that commonly closed in front with pins.[40]

Another option was the bed jacket, also known as the bed gown: a looser fitting garment that wrapped around the torso and was a little longer than a short gown. Fitted jackets were another option. Women generally wore a kerchief around their necks, more for warmth or protection from the sun than modesty.

Women wore petticoats (skirts) that closed with ties at the side. In winter, women could wear several petticoats for warmth. During river crossings while traveling with an army, women were particularly vulnerable, since the weight of the wet material and swiftness of the water could weigh them down. Crossing streams or rivers was not easy for women who followed the armies. Stockings for most common women were linen, referred to during that time as "thread," or wool. Stockings for upper classes were also commonly made of silk.

A variety of footwear was worn, including several kinds of shoes and moccasins. Some shoes were tied and others were buckled. Shoes—either leather or moccasins—were prone to wear out, especially with hard use, and replacing them was problematic.

Most women universally wore linen caps that covered their hair. While at first this might seem uncomfortable, it kept their hair clean and out of the way while working over a fire or doing other manual labor. Experimental archaeology of a sort supports this, as once they become accustomed to it, most modern female reenactors this author has spoken to prefer wearing caps.

The most common materials for clothing were linen, wool, linsey-woolsey and certain types of cotton. Silk would also have been worn by those of the upper classes. It was not uncommon for members of the lower classes, or "common sort," to have some secondhand silk garments. Other

Examples of clothing. The woman on the right is wearing a shift and stays, illustrating the undergarments. The lady on the left is wearing a gown, which was a common garment at the time. *Photo by Eric K. Williams.*

common materials were canvas and leather. While the people of the past wore more layers, it is important to remember that these were natural fibers that breathed, shed water and were quite comfortable. Aprons were almost universally worn by working-class females. They protected valuable clothing and could be used to carry items, and one could use the apron to protect hands when handling hot iron utensils and cookware.

Women, either civilians in the South or those attached to the armies, did not own a great deal of clothing. Unlike today, clothing was an important investment for people of the eighteenth century—it was expensive and valued. Often people only had one or two sets of clothes and perhaps one pair of shoes. When clothing wore out, was stolen or was ripped beyond repair, they were out of luck until it could be repaired or replaced. This was difficult for camp followers and refugees who were on the move or had limited access to supplies.

This woman is wearing a short gown, kerchief and petticoat, along with a linen cap. *Photo by Elizabeth Melton.*

This woman is in a bed jacket, apron and petticoat; she also has a straw hat. *Photo by Karen A. Smith.*

In a camp, women would have risen early with the troops, started a fire, cooked, cleaned, gathered supplies, prepared laundry and had other assignments. Their tasks might seem mundane, but they required skill and economy. Chopping wood, for instance, required maximizing their time and getting the job done quickly with as little effort as possible. Managing a fire is another skill: knowing when to add wood, how to build up coals for cooking and how to deal with uncooperative wind and weather are acquired proficiencies. Heavy pots and kettles had to be lifted and moved, often while still red-hot from the fire. Often made of cast iron, this also required skill and proficiency to avoid injuring oneself or others, or just simply to avoid dumping the contents of the pot.

A persistent myth has women's leading cause of death being by fire from working over a campfire or hearth and having her petticoat catch on fire. Recent research shows this to be a misconception, although those working near a fire had to be careful. Women who worked over fire learned safety measures, like taking a step back before turning so their petticoats did not sweep through the fire. Experimental archaeology suggests that holding the petticoats between the legs is also effective.[41] Disease, in fact, appears to have been the most common cause of death for women in the eighteenth century.[42]

Cookware of this period consisted of tin or sheet iron kettles. In stationary camps or forts, camp equipage was heavier, while lighter articles were taken into the field. Rations were subject to two variables: availability from supply lines and the seasons. In camp, cooking was often done by improvising: using a flat rock, a spade or flattened barrel hoops.[43]

Typical rations for a soldier (British or American) consisted of one pound of beef or salted pork, one pound of hard bread or flour, a pint of rice, a gill (four ounces) of peas, a gill of whiskey or rum and small amounts of salt and vinegar. Fruits and vegetables were added when available and depended on location and season. This was of course a best-case scenario—the armies that marched across the Carolinas often did not receive meat or bread regularly. The alcohol and vinegar were provided for health reasons and morale. Such a diet would have given an individual roughly 2,400 to 2,700 calories a day, which modern studies indicate is low for the rigors of combat. Female camp followers were to receive half the rations of a soldier; often they got a great deal less.[44]

Women also learned to cook by observing the food, as few had watches. In fact, people in the eighteenth century had a different concept of time that was not tied to a clock; the sun was used to tell time.

Laundry, perhaps the most common camp follower's chore, was generally done with wooden tubs, soap and some sort of scrub board.

Working over the campfire. *Photo by Karen A. Smith.*

Two types of soap were available: hard and soft. Hard soap was made from lye (leeched from wood ash) and grease or tallow. The soft variety was "like a clean jelly, and showed no trace of the repulsive grease that helped to form it."[45]

Laundry was sometimes hung over tents to dry, but more often over rope strung between poles in camp. Simple clothespins of split wood kept them in place. Making soap and washing laundry were big jobs, considering some camps could house several thousand men.[46]

These intangible skills are not recorded in the orderly books, accounts and family histories that tell us about women and their experiences while in the field with the armies. The descriptions of everyday tasks above give us a glimpse into the lives of the women who lived through these battles and add to the meager details we can collect about them.

Part II
Early Battles

The Revolution began in New England in 1775, but fighting quickly spread to other colonies. At first it was a civil war, as the civilian population took sides: some for independence (Whigs), others for the British (Tories). In time the small British garrisons that existed in the colonies at the war's start were supported by the arrival of large armies from England.

One of the war's first battles, at Moores Creek, illustrates the divided nature of the conflict. Women whose husbands were with the militias were drawn into the conflict. Later on, at Savannah, the regular armies fought and brought their camp followers with them.

In the three years between these battles, the two sides fought many engagements in the Carolinas and Georgia. This author has not yet found evidence of women participating, thus accounting for the large gap between 1776 and 1779.

Moores Creek, North Carolina

February 27, 1776

As one of the first military campaigns of the war south of New England, the battle of Moores Creek had far-reaching ramifications. In the fall and winter of 1775, law and order broke down in the colony of North Carolina, with Royal Governor Josiah Martin fleeing to a warship and asking for British troops to retake the province. He devised a plan to raise loyal Scottish troops and march them to Wilmington to meet the British forces. In the governor's absence, a provisional Congress made up of supporters of American rights was running the state and raising troops for its defense. This body was in communication with the Continental Congress in Philadelphia.

Large numbers of Scottish families resided in the Upper Cape Fear Region, near modern Fayetteville (then called Cross Creek). Facing hardships after the last failed rebellion against the English king in Scotland in 1746, many Scots here were reluctant to again rise against the British. Governor Martin had also forced many of these immigrants to sign oaths of allegiance upon landing in the colony before they could obtain land. An oath was a serious legal agreement in the eighteenth century, and these settlers were unlikely to act against it, regardless of personal feelings.

In January of 1776, thousands of Scottish men, as well as other Loyalists, gathered in Cross Creek for the march to the coast. This force met defeat in a pre-dawn battle on February 27 at Moores Creek, a swampy river crossing twenty miles above Wilmington that was fortified by the Americans. In less than five minutes, the Highlanders suffered about fifty casualties and were forced to retreat. In the following weeks, survivors were rounded up and arrested. The Americans were now firmly in control of North Carolina.

More importantly, the battle paved the way for events that were taking shape far to the north in Philadelphia. Having crushed an insurrection in their midst, the North Carolina assembly voted in April of 1776 to allow its delegates in the Continental Congress to vote for independence. It was the first state to do so.

Following the Loyalist defeat at Moores Creek, the English fleet arrived only to find no one to greet them. They prowled the Cape Fear River for some time, raiding plantations along the coast and battling with militia on the shore.

At the Kendal plantation in Brunswick County, "a few Women, who lived in the House, were treated with great Barbarity; one of which was Shot through the Hips, another stabbed with a Bayonet, and a third knocked down with the Butt of a musket." British generals Charles Cornwallis and Henry Clinton later sent money to the victims.

Records do not indicate what provoked the soldiers; perhaps the women tried to prevent their plundering the home, or the soldiers may have simply been releasing pent-up anger from previous skirmishes.[47]

One famous woman associated with the campaign is Flora MacDonald. She lived in Scotland at the time of the failed Jacobite Rebellion of 1746. Prince Charles Edward Stuart had attempted to overthrow British rule and become king of Scotland, but had met defeat at the Battle of Culloden. In the aftermath, Scottish leaders were persecuted and resistance was crushed. Flora was asked to help Prince Charles escape his English pursuers. In doing so, she gained everlasting fame among the Scots. Later Flora married Allan MacDonald and they immigrated to North Carolina in 1775.[48]

Flora's first language was Gaelic, though she later learned to read and write English (her name in Gaelic was Fionnaghal Dhomhallach). She had a better education than most in Scotland, but she was not part of the upper class. She was well mannered and apparently versed in proper social customs for a woman of her class and standing.[49]

While she did not participate in the march or battle at Moores Creek, Flora MacDonald was caught up in the events of 1775 and 1776 in North Carolina. Her husband Allan was an officer in the uprising that took place and led a detachment to Moores Creek. According to an eyewitness who knew her, when the Loyalist forces gathered at Cross Creek, "Flora came with her friends. I remember seeing her riding along the line on a large white horse and encouraging her countrymen to be faithful to the King. Why, she looked like a queen. But she went no farther than here, and when they marched away she returned to her home. She dined with us."[50]

Flora MacDonald, by Richard Wilson. *Courtesy of the National Portrait Gallery.*

Moores Creek Bridge. The bridge has been reconstructed at its original location. *Photo by author.*

The above account was collected by Benson Lossing from an eighty-seven-year-old resident of Fayetteville in 1849, who remembered Flora well. In fact, the woman had a note written by Flora that read, "February 1, 1776, DEAR MAGGIE: Allen leaves to-morrow to join Donald's standard at Cross Creek, an' I shall be alone wi' my three bairns. Canna ye com' an' stay wi' me awhile? There are troublesome times ahead, I ween. God will keep the right. I hope a' our ain are i' the right, prays your guid friend, FLORY MACDONALD." The elderly woman produced the letter, and she allowed Lossing to copy it.[51]

Other traditions mention Flora's presence when the army assembled, but most agree that she returned to her home and did not accompany them on the march. The preponderance of evidence makes it clear that she was there at the gathering but did not march to Moores Creek.[52]

Flora herself provides important details of the assembling army, noting that when they organized their numbers were "1600, having no arms but 600 old bad firelocks [firearms], and about 40 broad swords." This can be verified with other accounts to confirm that a lack of good weapons plagued the Loyalist army during the entire campaign.[53]

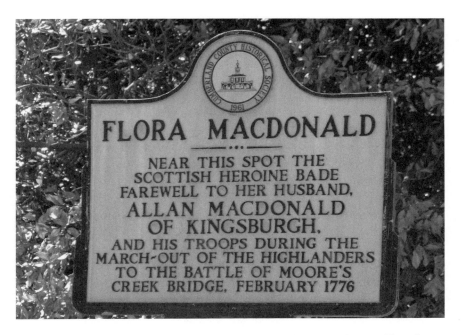

Flora MacDonald marker. This historic marker stands in downtown Fayetteville at the site of the Loyalist army's gathering. *Photo by author.*

Her husband Allan was captured in the brief but pivotal battle fought near Wilmington. After he was taken as a prisoner to Philadelphia, Flora would not see him for over two years. Flora remained in North Carolina with her children, and surrounded by enemies, she suffered greatly. She wrote that she was "deeply oppressed, and straggling partys of plunderers from their army and night robbers, who more than once threatened her life, wanted confessions where her husband's money was."[54]

In the spring of 1778, she managed to get to British-held New York City to be reunited with Allan. She then went on to Halifax, Nova Scotia, but her health began to suffer. She was about fifty-six years old and the strain of the last few years was taking its toll.[55]

Ill and having lost nearly all her property in North Carolina, Flora left for Scotland while Allan, still on duty, stayed in Halifax. On the return voyage, a French ship attacked her vessel, and Flora was wounded in the fighting. She lived in Skye for the remainder of her life, and died in 1790.[56]

Flora never wrote of her experiences, but she did correspond with people who recorded her story. Over time her tale has been retold by

Slocumb graves and Women's Monument at Moores Creek. The graves of Ezekiel, *left*, and Mary, *right*, were moved to the park in the 1920s. Behind them stands a monument dedicated to the women of the Lower Cape Fear. *Photo by author.*

many historians; however, they have often exaggerated her exploits, or confused her and Allan with another family. In fact, by 1909 there were four spots near Cross Creek designated as where she had lived. As stories were collected by historians in the nineteenth century, Flora emerged as a source of pride for the ethnic Scots of North Carolina, and everyone wanted to be associated with her. One historian has noted, "Ironically… it is in North America, which she came to hate most bitterly, that Flora is most lovingly remembered."[57]

While there were probably no women present at the time of the engagement, Moores Creek is one of the few battlefields with a monument to women of the Revolution (Guilford Courthouse, also in North Carolina, does as well). Known as the Women's Monument, it is dedicated to Mary Slocumb and the women of the lower Cape Fear River Valley who assisted with the Revolutionary effort.

Mary Slocumb lived about sixty-five miles northeast of the battle site with her husband Ezekiel. According to Elizabeth Ellet, who collected stories about women in the mid-nineteenth century, Mary had a terrible dream that motivated her to go to the battlefield. Unfortunately, Ellet does not name her source for this story, as she usually does. She often spoke to local residents or family descendants to obtain her stories; perhaps that was the case here.

This is how Ellet recorded the events, told in the first person by Mary:

I went to bed at the usual time, but I could not sleep. As I lay-whether waking or sleeping I know not—I had a dream, yet it was not all a dream…I saw distinctly a body wrapped in my husband's guard-cloak, bloody, dead, and others dead and wounded on the ground about him. I saw them plainly and distinctly. I uttered a cry and sprang to my feet…and so strong was the impression on my mind that I rushed in the direction that the vision appeared, and came up against the side of the house…I gazed in every direction…everything was still and quiet. My child was sleeping, but my woman was awakened by my crying out, or jumping on the floor. If ever I felt fear it was at that moment…I said aloud, "I must go to him." I told the woman I could not sleep and would ride down the road…I merely told her to lock the door after me, and look after the child. I went to the stable, saddled my mare…and in one moment I was soon tearing down the road at full speed. Again and again I was tempted to turn back, but I was soon ten miles from home. I knew the general route our little army was expected to take…The sun must have been well up, say eight or nine o'clock when I heard a sound like thunder which I knew must be cannon. It was the first time I ever heard a cannon. I stopped still. Presently the cannon thundered again, the battle was then fighting. "What a fool" thought I, "my husband could not be dead last night, and the battle only fighting now! Still, as I am so near, I will go and see how they come and see how they come out." So away we went, faster than ever, and soon I found by the noise of the guns that I was near the fight. Again I stopped; I could hear muskets, I could hear rifles, and I could hear shouting. I spoke to my mare and dashed on in the direction of the firing and shouts, now louder than ever. The blind path I had been following brought me into the Wilmington road leading to Moores Creek Bridge, a few hundred yards below the bridge. A few yards from the road, under a cluster of trees, were lying, perhaps, twenty men. They were wounded, I knew the spot, the very trees; and the position of the men I knew, as if I had seen it a thousand times. I had seen it in my dream all night!…there, wrapped in his bloody guard-cloak, was my husband's body! How I passed the few yards from my saddle to his place I never knew. I remember uncovering his head and seeing a face clothed with gore from a dreadful wound across the temple.

I put my hand on the bloody face; 'twas warm, and an unknown voice begged for water. A small camp kettle was laying near, and a stream of water was close by. I brought it, poured some into his mouth, washed his face, and behold it was Frank Cogdell! He soon revived and could speak. I was washing the wound in his head. Said he, "it is not that, it is that hole in my leg that is killing me." I took his knife, cut away his trousers, and stocking, and found the blood came from a hole shot though and through the fleshy part of his leg. I looked about and could see nothing that looked as if it would do for dressing wounds but some near leaves. I gathered a handful and bound them tight to the holes and the bleeding stopped. I then went to the others…I dressed the wounds of many a brave fellow who did good fighting long after that day. I had not inquired for my husband, but while I was busy Caswell came up. He appeared very much surprised to see me, and was, with his hat in his hand, about to pay me some compliment, but I interrupted him by asking, "where is my husband?" "Where he ought to be, madam, in pursuit of the enemy. But pray" said he, "how came you here?" Oh I thought! Replied I "you would need nurses as well as soldiers. See! I have dressed many of these good fellows…" Just then I looked up and my husband, as bloody as a butcher and muddy as a ditcher, stood before me. "Why Mary!" he exclaimed, "What are you doing there?" I could not tell my husband what brought me there. I was so happy, and so were all. It was a glorious victory, and I came just at the height of the enjoyment. It was night again before all our excitement had all subsided. Many prisoners were brought in, and among them, some very obnoxious, but the worst of the tories were not taken prisoners. They were, for the most part, left in the woods and swamps wherever they were overtaken. I begged for some of the prisoners, and Caswell readily told me none should be hurt but such as had been guilty of murder or house burning. In the middle of the night I again mounted my mare and started home. Caswell and my husband wanted me to stay till the next morning, and they would send a party with me, but no, I wanted to see my child, and told them they could send no party who could keep up with me. What a happy ride I had back! And with what joy did I embrace my child as he was to meet me!

The story starts to unravel upon further investigation. Ezekiel Slocumb did serve in the Revolution, but his pension application does not mention Moores Creek. This is reason to be suspect, since Moores Creek was such an important early victory that anyone who was there would be sure to mention it in his statement. Many soldiers who were on their way to

Moores Creek or serving in the vicinity say so in their pension applications. Ezekiel Slocumb only claims to have served from April 1780 to August 1781, and the only battle he names is Camden (Moores Creek was fought in 1776).[58] In addition, no one by the name of Frank Cogdell is known to have fought at Moores Creek. A search of various sources did not reveal his name.

Also, both Mary and Ezekiel would have been only sixteen years old in 1776 (he himself says he was born in 1760). While it is possible for them to be married and have had children by then, it seems unlikely. The legend also states that Mary left her infant son that night. Their only child, Jesse, was born in 1780.[59]

Examining details in the story reveals more problems. In her recounting, Mary explains, "I knew the general route our little army expected to take." If she did know where the militia was headed, she would have had a hard time keeping up with them. The militia under Caswell initially marched toward Rockfish Creek near Fayetteville, then turned back to Corbett's Ferry, and finally went to Moores Creek.

Her story also mentions the militia fighting "regulars," while at Moores Creek there were only Loyalists, no British regulars. She also spoke to Caswell, who was surprised to see her there. Caswell makes no mention of her in his report, nor do any other commanders.[60]

Other details do not match. She explains that "the sun was well up" and that it was "8 or 9" in the morning when she heard the firing. The Loyalist attack was early, in the pre-dawn darkness, according to participants' accounts. She also mentions twenty wounded men, while the Americans only suffered two casualties in the battle.

Perhaps Mary performed her act at one of the other small battles fought in eastern North Carolina in 1780 or 1781. She confronted Tarleton and his cavalry at her home when the British army moved through the region in 1781. Her husband was serving in the militia at that time; perhaps this is when she made her late night ride.

In the 1920s, the graves of Mary and Ezekiel Slocumb were moved from their family cemetery to the battlefield. This was done at a time when graves were often moved to prominent locations like monuments, parks or battlefields. Documents in the park archives at Moores Creek indicate this was done "before historians could analyze the legend."[61]

It appears that Mary Slocumb was not at Moores Creek, but in every story there is a basis of truth. Who is to blame—Elizabeth Ellet? Perhaps, or it might be Slocumb herself. If she told her story to Ellet or someone in her family, she may have forgotten details and made mistakes. Mary died in 1836, over fifty years after these events. Time may have clouded her memory. Ellet claims to have received her information from a "friend of Mrs. Slocumb," whom she described as "one who enjoyed the honor of her intimate friendship." Unfortunately, she does not state precisely who the informant was or what their relationship was to Mary Slocumb.[62]

Regardless, the monument at Moores Creek stands as a tribute to American women of the Revolution. It is one of the few monuments at a battle site dedicated to women who supported the cause.

After failed British efforts at Wilmington, North Carolina, and Charleston, South Carolina, the war moved away from the South for several years. British leaders maintained hope, however, that large numbers of Loyalists here would rise and support them. All that was needed was a British presence and Loyalists would come forward to help retake the area.

In 1778, the British again turned their efforts south. In the intervening years the war raged with fury in the Northern colonies. In the South, Loyalists lay low; many were harassed, forced to cooperate with the Americans or exiled. With the war stalemated in the North, the British looked for a new opportunity to win what was becoming an expensive and unpopular struggle.

Savannah, Georgia

September 16–October 19, 1779

Landing at Savannah in 1778, British and Loyalist forces easily captured much of Georgia. British records indicate that many women accompanied the regiments that moved from New York to the South. The Twenty-third Regiment had 370 men, 59 women and 62 children. The Seventy-first Regiment, with 1,274 men, also had 119 women and 83 children. John Peebles with the Forty-second Regiment recorded that women washed clothes while with the army in Georgia in 1779. At the same time, the Thirty-third Regiment had 475 men, 62 women and 28 children. Other units would have had camp followers and children as well.[63] In fact, Lieutenant Colonel Maunsell, in charge of embarkation of British troops at Cork, Ireland, noted it was necessary to allow women onto the departing ships, or else the men would desert.[64]

With Savannah, Georgia, in British hands, the Americans lost an important port and the largest settlement in this lower colony. Retaking the city became the objective of a joint military operation between the Americans and their new French allies (France had joined the war against England—the first foreign nation to recognize the independence of the United States).

An expedition arrived in the fall of 1779 to retake the city. The American and French forces laid siege to Savannah, bombarding the British fortifications. In a bloody assault, the Americans briefly penetrated the British earthworks, but were driven out. The campaign ended as a failure and strained relations between the allies.

French Admiral Count D'Estang wrote of the siege in a journal. Several of his entries mention the civilian women caught in the bombardment. He wrote that in one instance "a daughter of Mrs. Thompson was killed...by a solid shot" (a cannonball).[65]

On October 4, he records that the bombardment began and that "this violent fire was fatal only to the houses and some women who occupied them." He also notes that T.W. Moore, a British officer, observed that the town was "torn to pieces by shot and shell, and that the shrieks of women and children were heard…Many poor creatures…were killed in trying to get in their cellars."[66]

The British garrison of 6,000 men also had 929 women and 877 children. These camp followers were attached to both British and Loyalist units, many of which had been raised in the New York City area and sent south with the expedition. Among the Savannah Black Pioneers (a locally raised unit consisting of runaway slaves) were 186 men, 96 women and 74 children.[67]

D'Estang observed refugees fleeing the city when they could: "Many women…left the city and presented themselves of their own accord at the French camp. It was necessary for us to take good care of them as they were unwilling to return."[68]

All three armies at Savannah—American, British and French—had camp followers, although little has been written about their presence. Those with the garrison were trapped in the city and endured the allied bombardment; the women with the besieging American and French forces could remain safe in rear areas behind the lines, attending to chores while the troops engaged in constructing trenches and moving artillery into position.

Part III
Spring and Summer 1780

As armies converged on South Carolina in the spring of 1780, the civilians of South Carolina were planting their crops. Flax, corn, wheat and increasingly cotton were grown on the small farms of the western, or Upcountry, part of the state. Along the coast, rice and indigo (used in producing blue dye) dominated on the large plantations.

Life in the eighteenth century followed the cycle of the seasons. Then, more than now, people's work and daily chores varied greatly depending on the weather, season and task at hand. Spring was the time of planting and chores like shearing sheep for wool.

Not only did life follow cyclical rhythms in the eighteenth century, but the foods available to our ancestors did as well. Unlike today, different foods were available at different times of the year. Some foods familiar today were not yet grown in North America, or not available yet by trade.

Spring and summer vegetables included peas and green beans. Fresh berries in the summer included gooseberries, raspberries, strawberries, cherries and apricots. Spoilage was a serious issue, especially for armies in the field. Asparagus, for example, which appeared in June, had to be used quickly or else it spoiled; likewise with berries. Tree fruit like pears, apples and cherries could be dried and preserved. Yellow, or summer squash, was not yet grown by settlers.[69]

In late summer, melons like cantaloupe and watermelon, along with cabbage, carrots, cauliflower and turnips, were available. The following foods were not grown here or were largely unavailable at this time: grapefruit, summer (yellow) squash, zucchini and bell peppers. Tomatoes were not yet widely used.[70]

As the armies moved through the Carolinas, they would have supplemented their rations of salted beef and pork with these locally

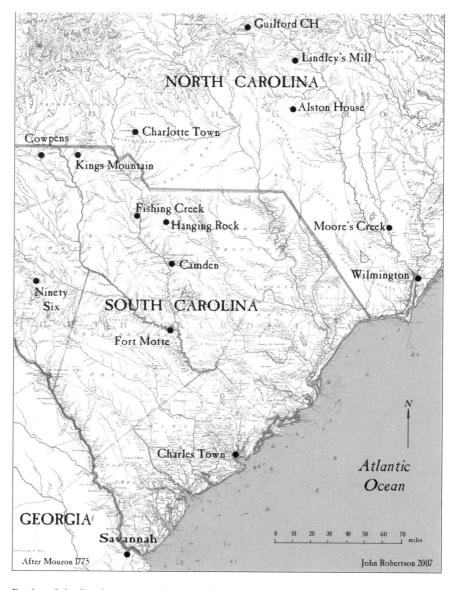

Battles of the Southern campaigns. *Map by John Robertson.*

available foods. These also would have sustained the militias operating in the area.

Charleston, South Carolina

April 2–May 12, 1780

In the spring of 1780, the British launched another effort at this important city, having failed to take it the year before. Sir Henry Clinton led 6,700 British, German and Loyalist troops against about 7,000 American defenders under General Benjamin Lincoln. With the armies converging on a major population center like Charleston, it is not surprising to find women caught up the military actions in and around the city.

Women were present with the British and German troops laying siege to the city, the same ones mentioned in the previous chapter. These camp followers had accompanied the army from New York to Georgia, and would remain with their units through the rest of the campaign. Also with the British forces were African American slaves, servants and runaways. Some British officers had servants with them who usually stayed in garrisons or secure locations. At Charleston, the entire army was camped north of the city as the troops laid siege; thus, servants of officers would have been present in the rear camps.[71]

One of the duties of those women that can be documented includes assisting the army's tailors in making trousers from newly arrived cloth. With the Loyalist units alone, there were 578 men, 19 women and 9 children. Many of the Loyalist women had been left in New York when the regiments left for the campaign.[72]

Wherever British troops went in America, slaves flocked to them as they hoped to gain freedom. The British employed the men in a variety of logistical capacities: scouts, pioneers (laborers), wagon drivers, musicians and even soldiers. Black women were present with Clinton's army, making cartridges, serving with the hospital and working with the artificers, who helped maintain equipment such as wagons and artillery pieces.[73]

General William Moultrie of South Carolina recalled that on April 3, before the British began their bombardment, "the women walk out from town to the lines with all the composure imaginable, to see us cannonade the enemy, but I fancy when the enemy begin, they will make themselves pretty scarce."[74]

As the siege dragged on, it became apparent that the Americans could not hold out for long. They were trapped on a peninsula with no chance of resupply or reinforcement. Both soldiers and civilians suffered during the artillery bombardment, and felt the pinch of few supplies. On April 13, a child and its wet nurse were killed by artillery fire. Moultrie wrote that on Monday, April 17, a woman was wounded by a cannonball in the city. That same day, a shell that struck a home killed a man and wounded the woman who was sleeping with him.[75]

Eventually the residents of Charleston became indifferent to the constant shelling. Lieutenant Governor Christopher Gadsden wrote, "Even the old women are so accustomed to the enemy's shot now that they travel the streets without fear or dread."[76]

With the American forces were many women who were attached to the Virginia, North Carolina and South Carolina Continental troops. There were, of course, many civilian women who lived in the city. All would be trapped and suffer in the coming bombardment.

The modern city of Charleston has grown beyond its colonial limits and now engulfs the area of the opposing artillery batteries. The American defenses stood at what is now Pinckney Square, as well as Vanderhorst, Hutson and Charlotte Streets (parallel with Calhoun Street). The most forward British trenches were located at modern Radcliff and Ann Streets. The colonial-era city occupied what is now bounded by East Bay, Calhoun and Pitt Streets (roughly half of modern downtown). These civilian and military casualties would have occurred within this confined space.

In the homes and communities surrounding the city, civilians began to feel the ravages of occupation. One incident in particular at Monck's Corner, about twenty miles from Charleston, stands out. British officer Charles Stedman wrote, "Some of the dragoons of the British legion attempted to ravish [rape] several ladies at the house of Sir John Collington, in the neighborhood of Monk's Corner." During this encounter one woman "was most barbarously treated; she was a most delicate and beautiful woman." Another "received one or two wounds with a sword…The ladies made their escape, and came to Monk's Corner, where by this time, Colonel Webster had arrived and taken command."[77]

Another account of the attack noted that Lady Collington and Betsy Giles's "Shrieks & Struggles" prevented the British soldier from "accomplishing his Designs," though some soldiers did steal from them. Next they went to the nearby home of Ann Fassoux and "made a Similar

Wall remnant in Charleston. This is the only remaining section of the tabby wall that protected Charleston in 1780. In the background is a statue of Francis Marion. *Photo by author.*

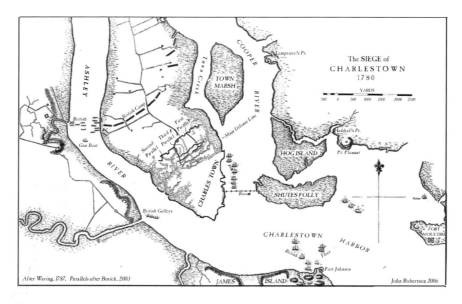

British and American siege lines at Charleston. The Americans, and the city's civilians, were pinned in the small, narrow peninsula. *Map by John Robertson.*

attack on her Person." In the struggle, they cut her "most sorely with his Sword" and "almost strangled her."[78]

Lieutenant Anthony Allaire of the British army also recorded the incident:

> *Three ladies came to our camp in great distress: Lady Colleton, Miss Besty Giles, and Miss Jean Russell. They had been most shockingly abused by a plundering villain. Lady Colleton badly cut in the hand by a broadsword, and bruised very much. After my friend, Dr. Johnson, dressed her hand, he, with an officer and twelve men, went to the plantation, about one mile from camp, to protect Mrs. Fayssoux, whom this infamous villain had likewise abused in the same manner.*[79]

Major Patrick Ferguson, who later led British forces at Kings Mountain, wanted to put "the dragoons to instant death." Once arrested, the guilty soldiers were "Tryed and whipped."[80]

Unable to receive supplies or reinforcements, and trapped on a peninsula with no way of retreat, General Lincoln surrendered his forces on May 10. This was the worst defeat of the war for the Americans, as it removed an entire army from the map. British forces occupied the city, and held it until the close of the war.[81]

Brattonsville, South Carolina (Williamson's Plantation)

July 12, 1780

The engagement at Williamson's Plantation in July of 1780 epitomizes the brutal warfare that raged across the state that summer. With British and Loyalist forces moving at will, American militia were often on the run, staying mobile and striking when opportunities presented themselves.

Loyalist officer Captain Christian Huck led raids through modern Chester and York Counties, gathering supplies and recruiting for the British forces. He was also ordered to "punish" the Rebels as much as possible. His primary target was the farm of militia leader Colonel John Bratton. Huck's dragoons stopped at many other farms on the way to that home, and encountered many women in the days leading up to the battle.

Due to the efforts of local historians and family descendants, the route and actions of Huck's raiding party are well documented. What follows is a detailed recounting of the days leading up to the battle at Williamson's Plantation. Naturally, events have been exaggerated and romanticized, and are clearly one-sided.

Huck's detachment left on June 10 from the British post at Rocky Mount, a fortified house overlooking the Catawba River near modern Great Falls, South Carolina. They first stopped at the home of Janet "Jenny" Strong. Mrs. Strong confronted the raiders while her sons were outside. Her oldest son, twenty-year-old Christopher, was in the militia, as was her other son, seventeen-year-old William. Two accounts, one hundred years apart, tell what happened at the Strong Farm.

A British officer reported that "two men with Rebell Uniforms were discovered running through a field of Wheat. The Militia fired upon them, killed one and wounded the other." The word "Militia" here means the Loyalist militia.

In the 1880s, local historian Daniel G. Stinson recorded a different version of the story. He wrote, "On Sunday morning, June 11th, the troops under Huck arrived at the house of Mr. Strong, near Fishing Creek Church. They immediately entered and plundered the house of everything, carrying away also the corn and wheat." After rudely speaking with Mrs. Strong, the account continues as Huck's men enter the barn,

> *where her son, William Strong, had gone shortly before their arrival. He had taken his Bible with him, and was engaged in reading the sacred volume. They shot him dead upon the spot, and dragged him out of the barn. The officers then began to cut and hack the dead body with their broadswords, when Mrs. Strong rushed from the house, pleading with all a mother's anguish, to the officers, that they would spare the corpse of her son. They heeded not her agonized entreaties, till she threw herself upon the bleeding and mangled body, resolving to perish as he had done by the cruel hands of her enemies, rather than see her child cut to pieces before her eyes.*[82]

This is no doubt a much more romanticized and embellished version of the story. Whether the boy was innocently reading his Bible or skulking in the fields near the home, Mrs. Strong had to bury her son William after the troops departed.

Next at the Simpson farm, the Loyalists looted and destroyed at will. Reverend John Simpson was an important local figure, and an outspoken Whig sympathizer. The reverend was not home, and his wife Mary confronted the intruders. They burned the house, and as soon as they were out of sight, she rushed in to save whatever she could. Frantically, she rescued two aprons full of books. In the process, Mary was severely burned, and spent four weeks recovering.[83]

Starting in late June, Huck led a larger force into modern York County, South Carolina, on another raid. On the morning of July 11, Huck's force arrived at the McClure residence. John McClure was a local militia officer, and his property and family were targets for Huck.[84]

Mary Gaston McClure was with her youngest daughter Mary, son James and Edward "Ned" Martin, husband of her daughter Olive. Two of her other sons were with the local militia. The men were melting the home's pewter dishes for musket balls. The Loyalists seized the two men, who were clearly aiding the enemy cause. They were taken prisoner and sentenced to be hanged the next day.[85]

Brattonsville, South Carolina (Williamson's Plantation)

According to family tradition, this is the dialogue that followed between Huck and Mary:

> *Huck stepped up to her and said, rudely, you see now Madam, what it is to oppose the King! Where are your other sons—John and Hugh? I should like to have them in company…We'll hang your son, Madam; that is his doom! Where are John and Hugh? Come, out with it! Search, men, they are hid some where—grand cowards!*
>
> *That is a lie! exclaimed the indignant mother, casting upon the brutal captain a look of intense scorn. You, sir, know better! You have never yet stood to meet them, and if John were here now, you would be afraid to face him!*
>
> *Damn him! cried Huck, tell me where I may meet him!*
>
> *To Gen. Sumter's camp, there you may possibly meet with him.*

At that point Huck, enraged, picked up the family Bible from the table and threw it into the fire. Mary sprang to rescue the book, and it was apparently kept in the family ever since. Huck then struck her with the flat of his sword. She commented, "Sir, that will be a dear blow to you!"

Upon leaving, the Loyalists set fire to the home. Mary ran in to rescue a sack of money. She then sent her daughter Mary to find the local militia and relay what had happened. Mary arrived late in the evening at their camp to tell of the capture of the two men and the devastation wrought by Huck's forces.[86]

Next, at the home of William and Mary Adair, the Loyalists were about to hang Mr. Adair, whose sons were in the militia, when some of the soldiers decided that he should not be held accountable for their actions. In the meantime, Mrs. Adair had her rings, shoes and handkerchief taken from her by the plundering soldiers. Captain Adamson of Huck's command spoke to Mary in private, telling her that she should convince her sons to join the Loyalist militia. She replied that her sons had a mind of their own, and acted for themselves. Adamson would meet them, in a sense, later at the Bratton home.[87]

It may seem strange for soldiers to want something seemingly impractical like women's shoes, which they probably could not use. When the soldiers were often truly desperate, some clothing could be used, and they could use many civilian garments and things like blankets and cloth. Of course, valuables like jewelry and money were always tempting targets. British officer John Andre wrote that sometimes looting was done "for the wanton pleasure of Spoil and which they have thrown aside an hour afterwards." This was often the case with pillaging done by both sides.[88]

Lastly, on the evening of July 11, the Loyalist troopers rode up to the home of Colonel John and Martha Bratton, located about ten miles south of modern York, South Carolina. John was out with the militia, and stopping at this home was a primary goal of Huck's mission.

A group of officers accompanied Huck to the plantation house, where they confronted Martha, who was alone with her small children, including son William. This young eyewitness later recorded the events that transpired. The Loyalists asked Martha if she knew where her husband was.[89]

When Martha said she did not know, an officer grabbed a grain sickle and placed it around her neck, saying he would "make her know." He went on to say that "if she did not immediately tell where her Husband was that he would cut her head off and split it." Her son John D. was six years old at the time, and recalled clinging to her petticoat while she confronted them.[90]

At this point, Adamson intervened, struck the officer and kicked him down the steps. He turned to Martha and assured her of her safety. Huck then asked to speak to her, and at first was "very courteous and polite." He even allowed young William to sit on his lap.[91]

Huck told Martha he was to offer her husband an officer's rank with the Loyal militia. Martha replied that she "had no influence with her Husband in such matters." He persisted, until she finally said, "My husband is in Sumter's Army, and I would rather see him die there, true to his Country and cause, than have him live a traitor in yours."[92]

Enraged, Huck "sprang up from his chair and stamped about the room swearing fearful oaths of vengeance against the Rebels, and my Father particularly." Young William recalled that in jumping up, Huck "threw me from his knee on my face on the hearth, and the result of my misplaced confidence will attend me to my grave in the shape of a broken nose."[93]

Huck ordered Martha to prepare dinner for him, and she did so. After eating, he had the women and children put into the garret as prisoners. The other children—Elisa, age thirteen, Jane age twelve, Martha, age nine, and Elisabeth, age one—were sent upstairs.[94]

Huck's force then moved a quarter mile to the west, to the home of James Williamson. The New York Volunteers camped in a lane near the home, while the Loyalist militia spread out in a field, their horses turned out to graze.[95]

In the meantime, the local militia, led by Colonel John Bratton, was closing in. Martha had dispatched, either before or after Huck's arrival, a slave named Watt to find her husband and deliver the news. In the early morning, the militia surrounded the camp and launched a surprise attack at dawn. It was over in minutes, as the Loyalists were caught sleeping.

During the night Martha and her children were upstairs, unsure of what the next day would bring. When gunfire shattered the early morning silence, Martha put her smallest children inside the brick fireplace. Musket balls were hitting the house, and one passed through a wall, hit the chimney and rolled along the floor. William, who was seven at the time, picked it up as a souvenir. Martha quickly pushed him back into the fireplace for safety. These details are from family history.[96]

When the fighting stopped, Martha heard someone enter the home and call out for her. It was John Adair, one of her husband's soldiers, and one whom Loyalist Captain Adamson had been looking for the day before. John found Martha upstairs and said, "Your husband has sent for you." Not knowing what this meant, and fearing he was wounded, she rushed downstairs. William, left behind and no doubt confused, began to cry, and Martha started to reach for him. Adair reached down to pick up the boy and told her to hurry. She met her husband, and was relieved to see him unhurt.

Martha had been summoned because the Loyalist officer Adamson, now a prisoner, had requested it. He had been wounded in the fight, and the Whig solders were going to kill him, when he asked to have Martha brought to him. She verified that he had helped her the day before, and he was spared. Martha and other local women nursed the wounded in the days after the battle.[97]

Local historian Maurice Moore, writing in the mid-nineteenth century, collected this account of Mary Adair's meeting with Captain Adamson that afternoon. The Adairs went to the Brattons' residence to be safer from further Loyalist harassment. "When the old lady saw him, she remarked, 'well Capt. You ordered me last night, to bring in my rebel sons, here sir, are two of them, and if the third had been within a days ride he would have been here also.' The Capt., a good deal chagrined, replied, 'yes madam, I have seen them.'" This was recounted by the son of one of those sons.[98]

The events at the Bratton and Williamson plantations were preserved not only through the writings of veterans, but also by the Bratton family. In addition to being recorded by William, the story of Huck's encounter with Martha Bratton was also recounted in an 1839 celebration at the battlefield, and preserved by the local chapter of the Daughters of the American Revolution later in that century. Local correspondents also shared the stories with historian Lyman C. Draper in the 1870s when he was collecting material for his Kings Mountain research. The raid and subsequent battle illustrate how civilians were caught up in the actions of armies in this part of South Carolina.[99]

The details of the raid and the events that transpired at the Bratton and Williamson homes are well documented, but no doubt romanticized. Initially family members who participated in the events told them to their sons and daughters. In time, these stories were passed on over the generations. By the mid-nineteenth century, local writers and historians began to record them. Unfortunately, we do not have many accounts from the Loyalist perspective.

Hanging Rock, South Carolina

August 6, 1780

After taking Charleston and eliminating the defending army there, the British were free to move across South Carolina and establish secure bases. British and Loyalist forces occupied Georgetown, Camden, Ninety Six, Fort Congaree, Rocky Mount and Hanging Rock.

Situated along the Great Wagon Road connecting Charlotte, North Carolina, to Camden, South Carolina, Hanging Rock was named for a nearby large boulder that overlooked Hanging Rock Creek. This flat, open plateau was an ideal place for an encampment.

The British occupied this site and established a post here, straddling the road and centered on the James Ingram House that stood here. The nearby post at Rocky Mount, overlooking the Catawba River, gave these two bases the ability to support each other.

That summer, American militia had been organizing and carrying out small-scale raids on the British and Loyalist forces that occupied the area. In late July, General Thomas Sumter attacked Rocky Mount, but was beaten back. He next turned to the nearby post at Hanging Rock. Accompanying the army was a thirteen-year-old named Andrew Jackson. Jackson's story reflected that of many caught up in the war. His brother, father, uncle and cousins were all serving. Naturally, the women of the family did what they could to support them.

The militia that attacked here under Sumter probably did not have any women accompanying them; they were traveling light and had been in the field for some time. Local women no doubt had visited them in their camps along the Catawba River in present-day York, Chester and Lancaster Counties of South Carolina.

Records do not indicate if any women were present with the Loyalist garrison, but there may have been. Under the command of Colonel

Hanging Rock Battlefield. This was the site of the Loyalist campsite, where the army's camp followers would have sought shelter during the battle. *Photo by author.*

John Carden, the garrison consisted of North and South Carolina Loyalist militia units, troops from the Prince of Wales Regiment and a three-pound cannon. The Carolina militia may have had women attached to them or visiting them, as some were local. The Prince of Wales Regiment, from New York and Connecticut, had women on its rolls when it came to the South.

One possible woman in the battle was the wife of Loyalist soldier . Samuel Burke, a free black from Charleston. She was a "free Dutch mulatto" who accompanied her husband Samuel with the Prince of Wales Regiment. After the war, Samuel wrote that she "accompanied him in all his marches and battles—during upwards of eight years in hard Service in action." His words pay an equal tribute to the women of both sides during the war. Burke did fight at Hanging Rock; thus, it is possible that his wife was here in the camp.[100]

Sumter's forces attacked the camp in what turned out to be a poorly executed assault. Initially they drove the Loyalists back; however, Carden's men counterattacked, and the fighting was hand to hand at times. Eventually the Americans overran most of the camp, but Loyalist reinforcements arrived. With many of his men plundering and some getting drunk, Sumter ordered a retreat.

Andrew Jackson's mother, Elizabeth, and her niece, Christina Crawford, rode out to the battlefield to look for Christina's wounded husband, James. He had been left on the field by Andrew and other relatives who could not carry him in the hasty retreat. James was still alive, though a Loyalist relative had stolen his coat.[101]

Many of the American wounded were taken to either homes in Charlotte or the nearby Waxhaw Presbyterian Church. Esther Walker treated her wounded brother, Joseph Gaston, in the days after the battle. That day she lost three other brothers—Robert, Ebenezer and David— and her cousin, Captain John McClure.[102]

One woman who had an impact on the battle was Jane Thomas, wife of Colonel John Thomas of the Ninety Six District. Governor Rutledge of South Carolina had sent ammunition into the backcountry to be staged at various points for the militia to use. One such cache was at the Thomas's house. A group of Loyalists attacked, trying to capture this valuable supply. The only people in the home at the time were Jane, her daughter and one soldier, Josiah Culbertson. The three held off the attackers, loading and firing through the windows of the home. The powder that was saved was later used by Sumter's army at Hanging Rock and Rocky Mount.[103]

While Hanging Rock was a large militia battle fought between American and Loyalist irregular forces, larger armies were maneuvering in the area. The next major battle happened just two weeks later, and fifteen miles away.

Camden, South Carolina

August 16, 1780

C amden, an important crossroads town, had been taken by the British earlier that summer. Many women accompanied the main British army under Cornwallis as it marched across the Carolinas, and were in the camp at Camden. Tarleton speaks of female camp followers, but offers no details. It is known that the Twenty-third, Thirty-third, Seventy-first and other regiments at Camden had women and children attached to them. Here Cornwallis likely would have left most of the army's women and baggage while his troops moved out to engage the approaching Americans.[104]

In the meantime, the Americans had organized a second Southern army to replace the one lost at Charleston. General Horatio Gates moved south through North Carolina with his force of Maryland and Delaware Continental soldiers, and militia from the Carolinas and Virginia.

The American forces moved south through a region of North Carolina devoid of supplies. The troops, and those accompanying them, suffered greatly on the march. There was little forage in this area, and the army was, according to one soldier, "living chiefly on green apples and peaches." The July and August heat also took its toll. A Delaware soldier wrote, "At this time we were so much distressed for want of provisions that we were fourteen days and drew but one half pound of flour."[105]

On the evening of August 15, Gates had his army begin a night march down the road to Camden. That same night, Cornwallis had his forces move out of Camden on the very same road. The two armies collided around two o'clock in the morning and in the moonlight amid the tall pines on both sides of the sandy road, a confused battle ensued. The forces settled down and waited for dawn. Many women were with the American Continental regiments from Maryland and Delaware, and there were likely some with the North Carolina and Virginia militia as well. Before departing for the South, the Maryland regiments averaged about 1 woman for every 16 men (in May, just three months prior to the battle of Camden, the Maryland regiments had 2,935 men and 170 women on the muster rolls). Many of them would have been present at Camden.[106]

Among those women was Mary Moore, whose husband Stephen was a sergeant with the Continental troops. After the war, with her husband dead, she petitioned the state of North Carolina for financial assistance. She wrote that "your petitioner hath during the late War performed many signal Services well known to many of the members of this assembly to the Cause of the United States of America in Saving many Hundred thousand pounds at Gates's Def[eat] hitherto has had no manner of Compensation for the Same."[107]

Gates had ordered the heavy baggage, "as well as a part of the women and children following the camp," to proceed to Charlotte, well out of harm's way. Yet "the women and children clung to their protectors." They stayed with the army, close to husbands and safety with the soldiers.[108]

At sunrise, the British attacked and managed to hit the weakest part of the American line: the militia. While the Continental troops fought well, the militia fled, and the Continental regiments became surrounded. Eventually they were overrun; it was a complete rout. Banastre Tarleton's cavalry was now turned loose on the fleeing survivors.

General William Moultrie, still a prisoner of the British in Charleston, wrote of the aftermath: "The cavalry pursued the fugitive militia, upwards of twenty-five miles, and made a dreadful slaughter among them; the road on which they fled was strewn with arms [weapons], wagons, the sick, wounded, and dead."[109]

A Continental officer wrote of the battle, and described the aftermath. "The retreat now became general, and the militia, by this time six or eight miles in the rear, some of whom together with our camp women, waggoners, and some scattering light horse, plundered all our baggage." For over twenty miles behind the army on the road leading back to Charlotte, stragglers, camp followers, wagons, horses and debris littered the road.[110]

Another account of the battle by North Carolina militiaman Guilford Dudley recalled his experiences in the retreat.

> *Passing the few wagons by the road side…I pushed on with the stragglers and soon overhauled several others that were ahead with camp-women, upon the top of the baggage, of which useful commodity*

Camden battle site. The modern road closely follows the historic road that bisected the battlefield in 1780. This view looks to the south, where the British attacked from. After overrunning the American troops here, they pursued them and encountered the fleeing camp followers farther up on the road. *Photo by author.*

> *it was said the Maryland line contained four hundred. The waggoners, having taken the alarm from the flying troops, drove on at full speed, and now and then coming in contact with a stump overset, when away went the camp-women, dashed twelve or fifteen feet, and some of them with new-born infants in their arms, a sight lamentable to view.*[111]

Dudley's account confirms several things: first, there were large numbers of women, especially with the Maryland Continental troops; secondly, the problem of women riding on the baggage wagons, a common occurrence and one that Generals Greene and Washington tried without success to control throughout the war; finally, the presence of many infants, confirming that not just women but entire families were traveling with the army.

Unfortunately, research has not found any accounts of women with the British forces. These camp followers likely stayed behind in Camden while the troops moved out to meet Gates's army. The Americans were moving south with their whole force, which explains why women were with the baggage on the road just behind the fighting.

Kershaw House. The reconstructed house sits at the site of the colonial town of Camden. Here the British army camped in 1780 and 1781. In the foreground is a redoubt, or earthen fort. *Photo by author.*

Camden may very well have been one of the most terrifying events for the women attached to the American army in the South. Caught up in the retreat, panic is contagious, and with the soldiers broken and in disorder, no doubt the women would have felt the terror and confusion. As British cavalry charged into their midst and began slashing at soldiers and civilians, it was no doubt a frightening retreat from the battlefield. An equally taxing experience awaited those who missed the Camden disaster.

Fishing Creek, South Carolina

August 18, 1780

Only two days after Camden, there was a second stunning British victory at Fishing Creek. General Sumter had been in the area of the Catawba River since the battles at Rocky Mount and Hanging Rock. With a small group of Maryland Continental troops detached from Gates's main army and his local Carolina militia, he made a camp at Fishing Creek, feeling safe from attack.

Tarleton, however, was rapidly approaching to strike him. The British cavalry rode up to a hill and could overlook the American camp. Sentries guarding Sumter's camp were not posted out far enough to give proper warning. The Americans were caught entirely off guard when the British arrived. Not hesitating a moment, Tarleton charged in a bold, sudden attack that was becoming his trademark style.

According to local Chester County, South Carolina historian Daniel Stinson, a young woman informed Tarleton of where Sumter was camped. Sarah Featherstone was a Loyalist who pointed out the location of the American campsite. Sarah apparently never married, and lived into the 1820s in Chester County. Tarleton himself does not mention her in his memoirs.[112]

Joseph McJunkin, an officer who was not present at Fishing Creek but got his information from someone who was, wrote that two "Tory Women" passed Sumter's campsite and then encountered the British approaching. The informant continues, "They gave Tarleton precise information as to Sumter's position and the arrangement of things connected with his army. They also informed him of a way by which he could leave the main road and fall into a road leading to Sumter's position at right angles to the main road." One of these women may have been Sarah Featherstone.[113]

It had been an extremely hot day, and the mood was relaxed in the American camp that afternoon. Some men were bathing in the river, and others were eating. Sumter himself was sleeping. The women in the camp may have been relaxing as well, or perhaps doing routine chores in this quiet downtime. Suddenly and without warning, the British cavalry attacked, throwing the camp into confusion. Panic spread rapidly.

There were several women in Sumter's camp when Tarleton struck. Elizabeth Peay, wife of a soldier named George, had followed her husband when he joined the militia. She was with other women who were fleeing as the British overran the camp. She had an infant in her arms and was sitting on a log with her other children when the attack began. Family tradition describes her and other women fleeing as the Loyalist dragoons were chasing them. At one point, she and her children hid behind a log as bullets flew overhead and struck the log they were hiding behind. Afterward, she found a wounded horse and rode to her former home in Virginia.[114]

Elizabeth returned to South Carolina later, when it was safe. She had fled her home with her children, as they had no food or supplies there. She represents the many women who, with nowhere else to go, attached themselves to the militia for safety and in hopes of steady food. She was twenty-six years old at the time, and lived until 1835. What we know of her comes from family tradition that was related to Lyman C. Draper. Elizabeth herself related the stories, and they were passed down in the family until they were recorded later.[115]

Another woman in the American camp, whose husband was killed, asked the British dragoons for some food. They replied she was a Rebel and deserved nothing better than the peaches growing in an orchard nearby.[116]

The above accounts are from letters written to historian Lyman C. Draper in the 1870s, and rely on local tradition. How many women were with Sumter at Fishing Creek, and in what capacity, may never be known. While the bulk of his army consisted of local militia, Sumter did have a detachment of one hundred Continental troops under his command this day. Some of the women may have been area residents visiting their husbands, or camp followers who were with the Maryland Continental troops.

Stallions, South Carolina

Summer 1780

This small battle illustrates how civilians were caught up in the bitter struggle that was now widening in the summer of 1780. The Stallion home stood east of modern York, South Carolina, off Route 5. Overlooking Fishing Creek, it had a first floor of brick and its foundations could still be seen in the 1870s. In the early 2000s, a large housing development was built on the site of the Stallion farm.[117]

This battle was typical of the guerilla war that raged among Loyalist and Whig families of the region. No British or Continental troops were involved, and the participants likely all knew each other. Like many small incidents, the date of the action is not known precisely; it seems to have been either June or July.

One version of this engagement is from a participant, Thomas Young, of the South Carolina militia. Young wrote that Loyalist troops had taken post at Stallion's farm, and local Whig commander Colonel Thomas Brandon led fifty men to attack it. They divided into two groups, sixteen under Captain Love (possibly Alexander Love) and the remainder under Brandon. Young was in Love's detachment, which approached the front of the home. Brandon led the larger group behind the house to cut off any escape.[118]

Mrs. Stallion was the sister of Captain Love, and Young wrote that she ran out of the home and begged him not to attack. Love replied it was too late, and she retired into the house, springing up onto the high doorstep.[119]

At that point Brandon attacked, and Mrs. Stallion was killed by a ball passing through the closed door. Love's men then rushed forward, and the Loyalist defenders returned fire. Surrounded and outnumbered, they soon put a white flag onto a gun barrel, but the defender was shot. Another white flag then appeared on a ramrod, and the Whigs ceased firing. Stallion, who in this version is a soldier under Brandon, was allowed to stay at his home and bury his wife.[120]

Another account of this event was told to historian Lyman C. Draper in the 1870s. This version has Stallion as a Loyalist. There is no mention of Mrs. Stallion leaving the house to talk to her brother. After the Americans opened fire, she tried to intervene and call for a truce. She opened the door, and Love himself fired and killed her, thinking that an enemy soldier would be in the doorway. This version has the Loyalist prisoners hanged by Love, who was enraged. The story told by Young has the prisoners taken to Charlotte.[121]

Christopher Brandon wrote of the battle in his 1832 pension application. He recalled that "Col. Love with whom I was at the time went up on one side of the house while Brandon came from the opposite direction. We commenced the assault, & after a number of rounds, the Tories surrendered. In the time of the firing, Mrs. Stallions, the sister of Col. Love, was killed."[122]

In another account, Brandon wrote,

> We surrounded the house at the distance of a rifle shot, before they knew of our approach; for not knowing they were pursued, they had posted no sentinels. We each got behind a fruit tree, and commenced firing through the cracks of the house, for it was a log-house, and some of the chinks had fallen out. The Tories closed the doors and windows, and returned the fire through the cracks, which served them as post-holes. This we found a losing game. Several of our men were wounded; but as the body of the fruit trees protected the center of our bodies, they did not wound us deep enough to kill.[123]

At that point a soldier rushed forward with a torch to ignite the house and burn the defenders out. Colonel Patterson was waiting to shoot at the door when it opened. Brandon continues,

> The door was suddenly thrown open, for the fire was penetrating the floor, and the sister of Col. Patterson, in wild alarm, sprung out, and at the same time exclaimed, "Why, John, do you mean to kill us all?" for she had seen and recognized her brother. The moment the door opened, Col. Patterson fired. He had no thought his sister would appear in the door. The ball passed clear through her head, and she fell dead. She was, said my old palsied friend, the most lovely and beautiful woman I'd ever beheld. She...had been married but a short time; & was well educated for the times in which she brought up. The Tories rushed out of the

burning house, and but few were left to tell the tale of their tragic end. Col. Patterson deeply mourned the untimely death of his sister, whom he fondly loved. He was guiltless of intending her the smallest harm—his finger was on the trigger when the door opened and thinking only of the enemies of his country, the ball had done its errand before he saw who first darkened the door. [124]

Lemuel Carroll, grandson of participant Thomas Carroll, told Lyman Draper in 1871 a version that had been passed down:

John Stallions was a Tory leader—sometimes had 150 men on scouts. His wife was a sister of the whig Capt. Love. The Whigs attacked his house early in the morning, surrounding it. Mrs. Stallions went to see her brother Andw. Love, in the orchard, & endeavoured to get him & party not to shoot at the house; & he tried to persuade her not to go back—but she went, wearing a sort of hat, as was the custom with her sex, & as she entered the door, probably mistaken for a man was shot through the head by some one on the opposite side from Andw. Love—she lived a couple of days. [125]

Francis Ross Miles, nephew of Andrew Love, wrote that her hat may have caused her to be targeted:

Col. Andrew Love died in Livingston County, Ky, on the Ohio River, near Smithland…The killing of his sister my aunt Love who married a man by the name of Stallions who was a Tory. There was a squad met at this house; my two uncles, Andrew & William Love attacked them at daylight. My aunt was getting breakfast for them to start, when the firing commenced she had on her husband's hat, put her head out at the window to tell her brother to stop she knew who they were, they knew the hat & fired at it—one ball took effect in the forehead. [126]

Several other statements by veterans mention the battle, but offer no details. None of the accounts give her first name; thus, we only know her as Mrs. Stallion. It is interesting to note the variety of details found in accounts of this one small engagement.

Part IV
Fall 1780

Autumn was traditionally a time of harvest and preparation for winter for the women of the Carolinas. Meat was smoked and salted for use over the winter, and fruits and vegetables dried and preserved. Foods by then available to cooks included radishes, pumpkins, onions, peaches, nuts, apples and wild grapes. For those living in the region, these foods came from their gardens, fields and surrounding lands. The army's foragers would have found these as well.[127]

With the coming of cooler nights, those women who were fortunate enough to have them began wearing cloaks or using blankets to stay warm. In their downtime, they would have gathered close to the campfire for warmth, especially as the evenings turned cooler.

Among the reinforcements sent to the South to bolster Cornwallis's army that fall was the Brigade of Guards, elite British troops. Orders at their disembarkation in New York stated that "Four Women pr. 50 Men may embark." These troops and their camp followers joined the main British force at Winnsboro, South Carolina, that fall.[128]

An example of women being subjected to discipline with the British forces under Cornwallis may be seen in his orders of December 27, 1780. "The Ordr. Respecting…Women, Servts., & other followers of the Army is repeated, any person who may be again found out of the Line of March, will be punished on the Spot, in the most Exemplary Manner."[129]

A quiet moment in camp. *Photo by Karen A. Smith*.

Kings Mountain, South Carolina

October 7, 1780

There were several women involved with the Kings Mountain campaign and battle, and one woman ultimately made it all possible. Much of what we know of these women comes from the writings of Draper. Other information comes from actual accounts of participants.

By the summer of 1780, the British had overrun most of South Carolina. The American Continental army was nonexistent after Camden; only the militia remained active to oppose the British.

Now counting on large numbers of Loyalists to rise up and join them, British Major Patrick Ferguson moved into the backcountry (western Carolinas) to recruit Loyalists. First at the fort at Ninety Six and then at other posts, Ferguson began to assemble several thousand men. As these Loyalists were armed and trained, his force moved into western North Carolina. In the meantime, the main British force under General Lord Charles Cornwallis occupied Charlotte, and prepared to move deeper into North Carolina.

At that point, the American militia organized to stop Ferguson. The young British officer had threatened to burn the homes of the frontiersmen if they did not stop resisting British authority. This galvanized the American militia, some of whom came over the mountains to meet Ferguson (militia from modern Tennessee, southwestern Virginia, western North Carolina, South Carolina and Georgia all converged on Kings Mountain). Hearing of their approach from two deserters, Ferguson began a retrograde movement to bring his army closer to the main British force at Charlotte.

As the militia assembled at Sycamore Shoals in modern Tennessee, the need for gunpowder became acute. Powder was a rare and precious commodity on the frontier, and it was desperately needed by the

American army. A local woman, Mary Patton, had been apprenticed in the trade of manufacturing gunpowder and contributed over five hundred pounds to the gathering army. Whether she donated or sold the powder remains unclear. Twenty-nine years old in 1780, Mary and her husband John had moved to the region from Pennsylvania. Born in Ireland, she had been trained in this smelly, and dangerous, skill. Mary lived until 1836, and was a local celebrity long after the Revolution. The battle of Kings Mountain may not have been possible without her.[130]

While Ferguson's army was at Gilbert Town (near modern Rutherfordton, North Carolina), a wounded officer, Major Dunlap, was left at the home of the Gilberts, who were Loyalists. Dunlap had apparently forced a young woman, Mary McRea, to stay with him. After Ferguson's army had departed, American militia came to the home, found Dunlap and executed him. What happened to Mary McRea, or where she came from, is not known.[131]

This story is supported, however loosely, by another informant who told Draper that he heard tales of a woman being taken prisoner by Ferguson's army while in the area. The author could not recall any more details about her or her fate.[132]

On the march through the Carolina frontier, Ferguson's army stopped at the homes of many Loyalist supporters. Dr. Uzal Johnson, who was attached to the army, wrote that they stopped at the Coleman farm near the Pacolet River in South Carolina. Johnson wrote that Mrs. Coleman was "a very warm Tory. She has two Sons in Coll Innes's Corps, She has a family of small Children...They have been greatly distressed by the Rebels for their Loyalty. The House stripped of all the Beds and other furniture, and the Children of all their Cloaths."[133]

Mrs. Coleman's two sons, Stephen and Prince, were fighting with the Loyalist militia. Later she was a refugee in Charleston, and records show she obtained coffins for her daughter and husband in December 1781. Charleston had become the only safe haven for Loyalist civilians by that point, with British and Loyalist troops driven from the countryside.[134]

By October 6, Ferguson's army had taken position at Kings Mountain, a local deer hunting camp along the road that ran to Charlotte. The pursuing Americans were closing in fast, now only thirty-five miles away at Cowpens, a well-known cattle pasture.

After a brief rest at Cowpens, the Americans chose a strike force to ride all night through a pouring rain. They reached Kings Mountain around 3:00 p.m. the next day, as the rain was ending. The Americans dismounted and surrounded the ridge, attacking up all sides. In one hour,

Ferguson's entire command was killed, wounded or captured. Ferguson himself fell near the end of the battle.

On the morning of October 7, there were at least three women at Kings Mountain, among Ferguson's twelve hundred soldiers. The next day there would be nine hundred more men present, and one fewer female.

These women, and the Loyalist army, had spent a cool and damp night on the mountain. It rained all night, saturating the ground. Campfires would have been hard to start, and hard to keep going. Most of the people in camp probably spent as much time as they could under whatever shelter they could find. Many of Ferguson's army, including the women, probably did not see a sunset on the last night of their lives. The dampness would have penetrated the air, although accounts do not state that it was extremely cold that evening.

One of the most famous stories of women at Kings Mountain concerns the two servants of Patrick Ferguson. Most accounts collected by Draper in the 1880s refer to them as mistresses, but their true status is not known. The British army did allow women to serve as cooks and nurses; perhaps they were merely servants. Their names appear as Virginia Sal and Virginia Paul (or Poll, or Paulina).

One account from a resident of Lincolnton, North Carolina, who wrote to Draper in 1880 tried to give him details of her, including her name, but admitted that "I have forgotten." The writer had spoken to veterans and recalled from local tradition the story of a woman with Ferguson, but could not recall her name. "Perhaps it was Featherstone," he suggested. This is the only reference to a woman with this name, and it is probably an inaccurate memory, as no other accounts mention that name.[135]

Another informant who lived near the battlefield and wrote to Draper recalled that men who were in the battle told him that Ferguson had two women with him. The evening before the battle, one plaited his hair while the other sang to him. How these informants knew the activities in the Loyalist camp the night before the battle is unclear. It must be remembered that this story was passed from aging veterans to a younger listener, possibly decades after the event. As with all of the stories concerning the two Virginias, they were not recorded until one hundred years after the battle. Over time the transmission of information was no doubt skewed and romanticized.[136]

Where these women came from and why they attached themselves to the British army is not known. Throughout the 1870s and 1880s, when Draper was collecting information for his book, his informants called these women "mistresses." Accounts of these women collected at the time

Campsite at Kings Mountain. The monument stands at the site of Ferguson's army's campsite. *Photo by author.*

reflect a very Victorian judgment of these women who were unmarried and attached to Ferguson. In fact, writers spoke of Ferguson as a very "immoral" man for having these two ladies with him. It is difficult to learn much about these women, as most of the writings were done by very disapproving writers who were more concerned with character than describing facts and details.[137]

All we know of the two Virginias comes from these writings; they do not appear in any primary sources but one. Many of those who wrote to Draper lived near the battlefield and had talked to veterans. Some were grandchildren of soldiers who fought there, and at least one had toured the battlefield with a soldier who fought there. Unfortunately, the gap of time between the event in 1780 and the stories being recorded in the 1880s no doubt skewed information and lost details.

During the battle, Virginia Sal was killed, and the other Virginia taken prisoner. Sal and Ferguson were buried in a grave at the foot of the hill. A necklace of glass beads was taken from Virginia Sal's body by one of the local soldiers. It was held by a local family in York County, South Carolina, as a relic of the battle. The traditions recorded by Draper do not give a better description of the necklace, and its current whereabouts are unknown.[138]

In 1845, Dr. James Tracy of the town of Kings Mountain went to the battle site with an elderly resident who had visited the site the day after the battle. The older man showed Tracy the site of Ferguson's grave, and the doctor proceeded to dig and found two skeletons, one male and one female. In 2000, the park did a ground-penetrating radar test that also showed what appear to be two burials at Ferguson's Grave.[139]

After Ferguson was shot from his horse, Virginia Paul was seen taking something out of his pocket. What the item was has not been recorded. Local traditions also stated that after the fighting was over, she rode around the battlefield on her horse, apparently unconcerned with what had happened to her army or her uncertain fate. Again, these were all stories collected by Draper from descendants of soldiers at the battle and local historians.[140]

Militiaman John McQueen mentions a woman in his pension application; he is the only eyewitness to describe a woman on the battlefield. He states that "there was a woman who Ferguson had been keeping who had left the British army and had come with news to Capt. Lewis, and she told him, that Ferguson could be known, by his using his sword in his left hand, as he had been wounded previously in the right."[141] Was this Virginia Paul, or one of the female prisoners in the Loyalist camp who made her escape during the battle? While

Graves at Kings Mountain. The marker calls attention only to Major Patrick Ferguson, but Virginia Sal is buried here too. Archaeological testing in 2000 confirmed accounts of her burial here. *Photo by author.*

many historians theorize that McQueen is referring to Paul, it is not quite clear.[142]

After about forty-five minutes of intense combat, the Loyalists were surrounded and surrendered. Ferguson had been killed, and the dead and wounded lay scattered across the ravines and hillsides. Both victors and prisoners camped on the battlefield that night.

Virginia Paul was now a prisoner—the only female prisoner among the roughly six hundred Loyalists held under guard that evening. Where did she sleep, was she separated somehow, how was she treated as one woman among all these soldiers? To these questions we have no answers. The next day, the troops quickly buried the dead and prepared to move out.

Sixteen-year-old James Collins, a private with the South Carolina militia, recalled the day after the battle: "Next morning, which was Sunday, the scene became really distressing; the wives and children of the poor Tories came in, in great numbers. Their husbands, fathers, and brothers lay dead in heaps, while others lay wounded or dying; a melancholy sight indeed!"[143]

The names of most of the local women who came to nurse the wounded and look for relatives remain largely unknown. Some of those whose identities have been recorded include Elizabeth Moore. Her husband William was badly wounded in the battle and had a leg amputated in the field. Hearing the news, his wife in Virginia mounted her horse and rode over the mountains alone, nearly three hundred miles, to find him. She nursed him back to health and brought him home. This story was told to Draper by the grandson of William and Elizabeth.[144]

Preston Goforth, who lived near the modern town of Kings Mountain, fought with the American militia and was killed in the battle. Upon learning of her husband's death, his wife hitched their horse to a sled to retrieve her husband's body. Mrs. Goforth buried him in the family graveyard on the Shelby Road (modern Business 74, west of the town of Kings Mountain).[145]

Draper recorded that Ellen McDowell and her daughter Jane, who lived nearby and heard the fighting, came to help the wounded. The two women spent several days there, assisting the other local women who had come to the site. Ellen's husband William had fought in the battle. At the time, Ellen was about thirty-seven, and Jane was seventeen. Jane McDowell lived until 1850. Elizabeth Countryman and her daughter, also nearby residents, came to nurse the wounded as well. Nothing more is known about them.[146]

On the battlefield itself, the Americans hastily buried the dead the next day. All of the prisoners were taken north to the Moravian towns (near modern Winston-Salem, North Carolina) by the American army. Either at this point, or earlier in the march, American commander Colonel William Campbell turned the single female prisoner loose.

He is reported to have said, "She was only a woman, our mothers were women, we must let her go." Virginia Paul was given a horse and a pass and sent to the British army, at Landsford in South Carolina. Whether she made it there is unknown. British military records make no mention of her joining them.[147]

As the victorious American army marched away with its prisoners, anger grew in the ranks, as many men had scores to settle with some of the prisoners. Now that the war had dissolved into a cycle of violence and revenge, many looked to get even for earlier atrocities. On October 14, thirty-six prisoners were tried for crimes such as house burning, horse stealing, etc. Nine of the worst offenders were convicted and hanged. The campsite and trial was held at the plantation of Aaron and Martha Bickerstaff, near modern Rutherfordton, North Carolina. After the hangings, Martha cut down the bodies of the dead Loyalists and buried them.[148]

The diary of Loyalist Dr. Uzal Johnson notes the presence of women at this campsite, something that no other primary sources note. Johnson wrote,

> *Coll Mills, Capt Wilson, Capt Chitwood and six others were hanged for their Loyalty to their Sovereign. They died like Romans, saying they died for their King and his Laws. What Increased this melancholy scene was the seeing Mrs. Mills take leave of her Husband, and two of Chitwood's daughters take leave of their Father. The latter were comforted with being told their Father was pardoned. They went to our Fire where we had made a Shed to keep out the Rain. They had scarce set down when News was brought that their Father was dead. Here words can scarce describe the Melancholy Scene, the two Young Ladies swooned away, and continued in fits all Night. Mrs. Mills, with a Young child in her Arms, set out all Night in the Rain with her Husband's Corps, and not even a Blanket to cover her from the inclemency of the Weather.*[149]

When and under what circumstances the wives and daughters of these two prisoners joined the army is not known. Nor is it recorded if other women joined the army in the days after the battle. Unfortunately, the diaries of Loyalists like Johnson, Alexander Chesney and Anthony Allaire fail to mention women in the camp prior to the battle.

When the prisoners arrived in the Moravian towns of North Carolina (Salem, Bethabara and Bethania) that fall, no doubt they came into contact with more women among the civilians of the settlements.

Part V
Winter 1780–81

As fall turned to winter and the year advanced from 1780 to 1781, British fortunes were declining. While British forces were initially victorious all spring and summer, by fall the Americans had reorganized and struck back, most notably at Brattonsville and Kings Mountain.

The leaves were now down and cold air blasted the soldiers and camp followers who huddled in tents and shelters. For those in the field since the summer, clothing was wearing out and replacing it was not easy. The Continental troops and their camp followers received irregular shipments of cloth and garments. Militia and civilians were on their own to make, repair and more often steal and appropriate clothing and equipment.

It was not unusual for women to wear several petticoats to stay warm. Camp followers and soldiers huddled close around their campfires for warmth in the evenings. Sleeping out in the open, often with only blankets on the cold, damp ground, caused sickness in many.

Harsh winters with heavy snows were not uncommon during winters in the eighteenth century. The earth was experiencing what scientists have discovered was a mini ice age. As climates change over time, the 1700s were a period when winters were longer, colder and harsher than before or since. Rivers like the Hudson froze regularly, and even in the South, observers reported cold air, ice and snow. In these conditions the armies, and the women who accompanied them, battled the elements.[150]

Cooking fire. *Photo by Karen A. Smith.*

Cowpens, South Carolina

January 17, 1781

Perhaps few other battles in all of American military history were so complete as Cowpens. Fought on the cold morning of January 17, 1781, the battle likely lasted less than half an hour. In that time, a British force of roughly one thousand men lost over nine hundred. The American troops suffered about sixty casualties.[151]

The forces involved included a mix of militia and Continental troops on the American side, and British regulars along with the British Legion (Loyalist dragoons, or cavalry).

In the aftermath of the Camden disaster, General Nathanael Greene arrived to reorganize the American Southern army. With him came the experienced combat leader, General Daniel Morgan. While the British camped at Winnsboro, South Carolina, for the winter, Greene sent Morgan from his camp at Cheraw to engage the British.

In Cheraw, Greene's army could rest and refit. Some women were used as nurses at this time. Dr. James Browne wrote to Greene prior to the battle of Cowpens that he wanted to appoint and pay a matron for every one hundred sick men and to hire and pay nurses to "attend, cook and wash for the Sick."[152] The army also used local "country women" to make shirts and overalls (trousers that covered the ankles) for the troops. Greene also considered sending women into British-held Camden to sell provisions and spy on them.[153]

In the meantime, Cornwallis sent one of his ablest officers to meet Morgan's detached force. Lieutenant Colonel Banastre Tarleton hoped to strike quickly at General Daniel Morgan's small army in upper South Carolina. Tarleton's force was a light, fast-moving group, and he would have taken no women with him. Tarleton wrote to Cornwallis in early January discussing his advance, and specifically ordered that no women accompany him.[154]

Morgan had set up camp at Grindal Shoals, a well-known crossing point on the Pacolet River. Sometime around January 14, twenty-year-old Anne Kennedy of Union County rode into Morgan's camp to warn him of the British approach. Her father and uncle were in the militia, and would both fight at Cowpens the next day. Anne had often acted as a messenger, hiding notes in her stockings. She was not the only messenger reporting British movements, but she still conveyed vital information.[155]

Spreading the word that night throughout the countryside was Kate Moore Barry. Born in Ireland, she was twenty-nine years old in 1781. According to local tradition, with her husband and brother off in the militia, she tied her young daughter Kate to a bedpost and left home to help spread the alarm. What she did with her other children is not known. That night she passed the news for the local militia to gather at the Cowpens, a local landmark. Her husband, Captain Andrew, was in the battle the next morning.[156]

It was a cold evening to be out, especially riding alone through the countryside at night. Roads were poor, houses few and far between and the countryside held both friends and enemies: armed Loyalists were in the area.

Kate and Andrew had eleven children, and lived two miles north of Walnut Grove, the home of her parents. She died in 1823 and is buried at Walnut Grove, now a historic site open to the public near Spartanburg.[157]

Unfortunately, Morgan's official correspondence does not shed more light on these women. In a letter to General Greene, he only writes of receiving "intelligence" of the British approach.[158]

Morgan hurriedly fell back with his army and took position at a local cattle pasture, forever after known as Cowpens. He chose this ground not only because it offered a good place to make a stand, but also because it was a local landmark. All night long, militia came into the camp, swelling his numbers.[159]

At dawn, Morgan had his troops deployed in three lines. Just after sunrise, Tarleton arrived. As the British advanced across the open field, they met each line in succession, driving the Americans back. It appeared that Tarleton was winning, but it was a ploy. Morgan had instructed his troops to fire and fall back. At the third line, his best troops waited. After trading volleys of musket fire, the British charged, but were shocked by a sudden American counterattack. The British broke and ran; Tarleton tried to rally his men, but was soon forced to retreat as well.

After the fight was over, local woman Elizabeth Countryman and her daughter again helped bring water to the wounded, as they had done earlier at Kings Mountain. Many of the wounded were taken to local

Cowpens Battlefield at sunrise. Here, just after dawn on January 17, 1781, the Americans defeated the British. *Photo by author.*

residents so they would not be left out in the open, as it was a cold January. Mrs. Hicks and her daughter, who lived nearby, apparently took some wounded men to their home to treat them.[160]

As Tarleton and his surviving dragoons raced from the disaster, American cavalry pursued them. This was a chance not to be missed: the dreaded Tarleton was on the run and Lieutenant Colonel William Washington of Morgan's army wanted badly to capture or kill him (William was a cousin of the commander in chief, George Washington). Tarleton and a small number passed the Goudelock Farmhouse, where they briefly stopped. The home stood at a crossroads, and here they took Adam Goudelock and forced him to show them the way to the Scull Shoals on the Pacolet River.[161]

Moments later, when Washington's dragoons rode up to the house, Mrs. Goudelock chose to send them down the wrong road. She feared that if they caught up with Tarleton's party, her husband would be killed in the encounter. Washington raced off down the road that led to Grindal Shoals, where he failed to find Tarleton, but did manage to round up several British prisoners.[162]

If any women were at Cowpens during the battle, they would have been with Morgan's army. These troops spent a cold night camped on the ground, as there were few tents available. The camp was up early the next morning, before dawn, and began preparing for battle. The only women that can be documented were those who played parts before and after the battle. Thus at both the start and finish, women were involved with the Cowpens campaign.

Guilford Courthouse, North Carolina

March 15, 1781

After the stunning defeat at Cowpens (in which Tarleton lost nine hundred of the one thousand men he brought onto the field), General Cornwallis was furious, and hoped to regain the prisoners. He moved his army north to pursue Morgan into North Carolina. Morgan's forces united with those of General Greene and the Americans managed to stay ahead of the pursuing British, eventually reaching the Dan River in Virginia. Both armies had marched entirely across North Carolina. Cornwallis, unable to overtake Greene, retired to Hillsborough, where he issued a proclamation for Loyalists to rise and support the British army.

The march across North Carolina from the Cowpens area to the Virginia border was grueling for the British. The following are from Cornwallis's orders on January 30, 1781, as the army prepared to move out: "When the brigade marches, the women, and weak and sickly men, will march in the rear of the second battalion."[163]

The British army's camp followers lived in an environment with a strict routine. Typically they, like the troops, were up early and ready to march or carry out the day's assignments. Orders like this were not uncommon from January through March of 1781: "Horses to be loaded and troops ready to march at half past five o'clock tomorrow morning." The army was often marching by six in the morning.[164]

The intrepid British army marched over two hundred miles between the battles at Cowpens and Guilford Courthouse. During that time, the army endured rain and cold weather, crossed rivers and suffered from lack of supplies.

On January 28, the army's orders stated that "the Supply of Rum for a time Will be Absolutely impossible, & that of Meal very uncertain." Rum was part of a soldier's regular ration, and its disappearance was no doubt a source of discontent. The army subsisted largely on foraging, often eating corn. Those orders also stated that officers were to "Keep good Order & prevent Plundering" by the troops and the "followers of the Army."[165]

The following marching orders show how women could be caught in situations that require nontraditional acts from them: "In Case the Brigade Should be ordered forward…they will form a Guard to the Baggage, Packs, or what else May be left in their Charge."[166]

Resupplied and reinforced in Virginia, Greene reentered North Carolina and moved his army to a position at Guilford Courthouse, at the modern city of Greensboro (named in his honor). Cornwallis was anxious to force him into battle. While outnumbered and deep in hostile territory, the British commander felt the skill of his veteran troops could even the odds.

The British were desperately short on supplies in the weeks prior to the battle. Cornwallis wrote to Lord Francis Rawdon, "The fatigue of our Troops and hardships which they suffered were excessive." He goes on to note that "the Troops are in the greatest want of shoes and other Necessities." Officer Charles Stedman also noted that the army was low on supplies. Food was scarce, and clothing was in rags. No doubt the camp followers with the British army suffered equally as much. The army had been marching and camping out in the elements through January and February. It was also too early in the season for fresh fruit and vegetables to be available.[167]

The suffering is reflected in Cornwallis's orders on March 1:

> *The officers commanding companies, cause an immediate inspection of the articles of clothing at present in possession of the women in their companies and an exact account taken thereof by the pay Sergeants, after which their necessaries are to be examined at proper opportunities and every article found in addition thereto, burned at the head of the company, except such as have been fairly purchased on application to the commanding officers and regularly added to their former list by the Sergeants as above. The officers are…ordered to…prevent the women (supposed to be the source of the most infamous plundering) from evading the purport of this order.*[168]

Recently a local woman had been robbed of "a watch, a black silk handkerchief, a gallon of peach brandy, and one shirt." Plundering by the British army's camp followers was a problem that would not go away, and it continued through their entire stay in North Carolina.[169]

Discipline was mentioned in the following orders from Cornwallis on March 2 regarding plundering. He wrote that he was determined to "punish all men and women so offending, with the utmost severity and example." Frequent roll calls were implemented to discourage straggling and looting. Orders stated that "Women [are] to attend all Roll-calls in the rear of the companies, (except such as are in the service of officers) any and every one found absent to be immediately whipped and drummed out of the brigade." The army's women were also ordered to "attend all punishments" so that the message was delivered clearly.[170]

Just a few days prior to the battle of Guilford Courthouse, Cornwallis issued orders that included, "Pickets are desired to be very alert and particularly attentive to people that pass their party; no one must be suffered to pass but by authority from Head-quarters. Women particularly are to be attended to."[171]

On March 14, the British camped at Deep River Friends Meeting House, south of modern Greensboro (where modern Route 68 and Wendover Avenue intersect). The British army's female camp followers would have remained with the baggage in the army's rear when the troops marched out of camp early on the morning of March 15 to engage the Americans. Similarly, those women who accompanied Greene's army would have remained with their baggage and rear guard at Troublesome Creek, about fifteen miles to the north. This was his army's pre-battle assembly area and its rally point in case of defeat. No doubt the wives on both sides were anxiously watching as husbands marched out to do battle.[172]

Thus it seems that there were probably few, if any, women present during the fierce battle at Guilford Courthouse, as each army had left its baggage and camp followers behind to move forward with only the combat troops.

Accompanying Hugh Black from Maryland was his wife, Sarah. His pension statement notes that she was a washerwoman with the army. Hugh does not appear to have fought at Cowpens, but was at Guilford Courthouse, where he was wounded twice. If she was present at this time, Sarah likely would have remained with the baggage at Troublesome Creek while the battle was fought.[173]

The Americans deployed in three defensive lines near the courthouse. The British attacked and gradually drove the first and second lines back. Vicious fighting erupted at the third line, and eventually the Americans gave way. It had been a hard-fought battle, yet the suffering was not over for the two armies.

Soon after the shooting stopped, a heavy rain began, and continued for the next few days. Both armies, now exhausted, found themselves caught with little shelter. The wounded suffered terribly, and many died of exposure.

In the engagement's aftermath, local women came to nurse the wounded and search for relatives. One woman associated with the battle is Kerrenhappuch Norma Turner. Family tradition maintains that she rode three hundred miles from Halifax County, Virginia, to aid her wounded son.

Historical records, however, indicate that the bulk of the wounded were sent to homes and public buildings surrounding the battlefield. Protected from the elements and in the hands of civilians, they received better care this way. Thus, if Kerrenhappuch did journey to Guilford Courthouse, she may never have actually set foot on the battlefield, though she may have assisted the wounded in area homes or one of the nearby meetinghouses. A statue honoring her stands today in Guilford Courthouse National Military Park.

Kerrenhappuch's story is another that has become clouded over the centuries. Accounts have her being over 80 years old in 1781. It is possible that she could have ridden alone for hundreds of miles at that age, but unlikely. She is thought to have died in 1807 at age 115.[174]

There were many women attached to the army with the Maryland and Delaware Continental regiments that fought in the Carolinas for the remainder of the war. How many there were remains unclear, but military records and papers reveal several references to women and families. Greene's military orders refer to women receiving rations, obviously on the strength of the army.[175]

The British were not the only ones who suffered in the campaign. It had been a grueling march leading up to the battle for the Americans as well. Lieutenant Colonel Henry Lee wrote, "The shoes were generally worn out…clothes much tattered and not more than one blanket for four men."[176]

In the days after the battle, women in the British army assisted the many wounded. Cornwallis's army suffered severely, losing one out of every four men in the battle. He ordered that "all the women of the army except one a company, to be immediately sent after the wounded men of the army." This is revealing, since it makes clear that there were several women with each company.[177]

A few days later, on March 20, Cornwallis wrote that since the wounded had not been receiving adequate food, a detachment should go to the hospital to "inspect their kettles, appointing for this purpose those women that can be spared from other avocations in the Hospital, together with men under slight wounds to perform this duty for the rest." This makes it clear that the British army's women were treating the wounded in the days after the battle.[178]

Kerrenappuch Monument. This monument stands at the Guilford Courthouse battlefield. *Photo courtesy of Guilford Courthouse National Military Park.*

New Garden Meeting House. Here the British army's camp followers treated the wounded after the battle. *From* Benson J. Lossing's Pictorial Field-Book.

In the aftermath of the battle, Sergeant Berthold Koch of the German Von Bose Regiment wrote of the army's condition. "We remained on the battlefield for three days, under the open skies without tents…each man, officers as well as privates, received four measures of corn instead of bread and for meat, such cattle as the enemy had left behind…We placed the corn on the fire to cook it. Then it was taken from the container and eaten. The meat was either boiled or roasted on sticks and eaten." No doubt the army's camp followers also had to make do to cook and find shelter in these conditions.[179]

Records in the papers of General Cornwallis indicate that local citizens contributed supplies to the British wounded at the New Garden Meeting House, just a few miles from the battlefield and scene of an earlier skirmish. In fact, the names of wives of the wounded soldiers have been recorded. They include Nancy Safewright, Margaret Thornbrugh Cannady, Jemimah Uthank and her children, Elizabeth Hunt and her three small children, Anna Perkins, Hepzibah Macy Pears and Ann May. Mrs. May had a daughter, Miriam, on March 21.[180]

One incident near Guilford Courthouse reveals the brutal nature of the civil war that raged among neighbors in the region. John Alexander, his wife and daughter Jane lived in a cabin several miles south of the courthouse, near modern Pleasant Garden. Alexander was a Whig, and feared attack from his Loyalist neighbors.

A group of Loyalists came to raid their home. Led by a neighbor named Powell, they began to batter the locked door. Inside, John loaded his weapon, his wife grabbed an axe and Jane readied a pitchfork. Details are unclear, and different versions of the story have been passed down. One account says the Loyalists broke into the home and John fired, but his weapon misfired. Jane then stabbed Powell with her pitchfork. Another version states that Jane managed to stab and kill Powell through a crack in the wall. Both versions agree that she killed the leader. The Loyalists retreated, and buried Powell nearby (the area became known as Powell's Ridge). Powell was a neighbor, and one version of the story has John wearing his hat to church the next day as a trophy.

The event unfolded on what is today Minden Road in Pleasant Garden. As late as the 1990s, the cabin site was visible in a field that grew crops. Jane's pitchfork is currently in the Greensboro Historical Museum. There is no date or time frame given for this incident.[181]

Part VI
Spring and Summer 1781

Another cycle now began: spring. Planting and other tasks occupied the days of the region's farmers. Yet this spring saw changes in the war's course. As warm weather returned to the Carolinas, Greene prepared to invade South Carolina. General Cornwallis had taken his army to Wilmington to resupply and rest.

The men and women of both armies were feeling the effects of a year of active campaigning. Shoe leather wore out, clothing was torn and threadbare and the armies did not receive regular shipments of supplies. Garments were taken from the wounded, the dead, the captured and civilians. Devastation and interruption of work and transportation limited the supplies and food available to armies and civilians alike.

Laundry, along with sewing and repairing garments, was commonly done by camp followers. *Photo by Brittney Robinson.*

Fort Motte, South Carolina

May 8–12, 1781

The story of Rebecca Motte, like many heroines of South Carolina, has taken on a larger-than-life status. Here the best primary account of her actions, the writings of Lieutenant Colonel Henry Lee, will describe her role in the siege of Fort Motte. Writer Benson Lossing, who traveled through the area in the 1850s, encountered residents who knew her and recorded their impressions of her. These two stories make for an interesting comparison. Elizabeth Ellet seems to have relied on Lee's writings for her retelling of the story.

Rebecca Brewton was born in 1737 along the Santee River in South Carolina, the daughter of an English gentleman. She married planter Jacob Motte in 1758, and together they had seven children. By the time of the Revolution, Jacob had died and the widow lived with some of her children at the plantation overlooking the Congaree River. Rebecca's plantation produced rice, corn, beef, pork and other supplies that supported American forces during the war. She lived on her plantation after the war, and died there in 1815.[182]

The incident at Fort Motte is much like that at Brattonsville, where the story is well documented and quite famous, though romanticized and one-sided. While shrouded in myth and legend, the story is no doubt true. It is worth investigating, since Rebecca's actions directly affected events during the siege, and the capture of this post was important in securing the area for the American army.

Fort Motte was nothing more than Rebecca's plantation house, which Loyalists forces had taken over and fortified. Situated near the road to McCord's Ferry, an important crossing of the Congaree River, the site was an important post in the string of British defenses across the central part of the state. The home was apparently a three-story structure and sat on the highest point of land on a hill. Rebecca and her children moved to a smaller house on the grounds. American forces under Lieutenant Colonel Henry Lee and General Francis Marion arrived and laid siege to the house, digging trenches and placing artillery in position. The Loyalist garrison under the command of Captain Lieutenant Donald McPherson felt that they could hold out, and refused to surrender.[183]

The British had constructed substantial defenses at the house, including a moat and an earthen and wooden fortification that protected the first two stories of the home. Inside the earthworks were firing steps, so defenders could reload under shelter. A total of 184 British, German and Provincial (American Loyalist) troops defended the home.[184]

The Americans began digging trenches and working their way closer to the home in a classic siege process. They also built a mound for an artillery piece that they had. The work was time consuming, and Lee and Marion hoped for a faster solution.[185]

Lee writes of the incident involving Rebecca, "The large mansion in the centre of the encircling trench, left but a few yards of the ground within the enemy's works uncovered; burning the house must force their surrender."[186] While some soldiers kept digging their approach trenches forward, others began preparing combustible materials to fire the home. Lee called the measure "reluctantly adopted" and "repugnant."[187]

Mrs. Motte had allowed Lee use of her temporary house as his headquarters. He writes of her hospitality during the siege, noting her "richly-spread table." Her "active benevolence found its way to the sick and to the wounded; christening with softest kindness infirmity and misfortune."[188]

Lee continues, "Taking the first opportunity which offered, the next morning, Lieutenant-Colonel Lee imparted to Mrs. Motte the intended measure; lamenting the sad necessity, and assuring her of the deep regret which the unavoidable act excited."[189]

> [Rebecca] *gave instant relief to his agitated feelings, by declaring, that she was gratified with the opportunity of contributing to the good of her country, and that she would view the approaching scene with delight. Shortly after, seeing accidentally the bow and arrows which had been prepared, she sent for the lieutenant-colonel, and presenting him with a bow and its apparatus imported from India, she requested his substitution of these, as probably better adapted for the object than those we had provided.*[190]

Rebecca Motte. *From* Benson Lossing's Pictorial Field-Book.

Lee writes, "The lines were manned, and an additional force stationed at the battery, lest the enemy, perceiving his fate, might determine to risk a desperate assault, as offering the only chance of relief." One last time, the Americans offered the garrison a chance to surrender, and again they refused.[191]

"It was now about noon," Lee recalled, "and the rays of the scorching sun had prepared the shingle roof for the projected conflagration. The first arrow struck, and communicated its fire; a second was shot at another quarter of the roof, and a third at a third quarter; this last also took effect; and like the first, soon kindled a blaze."[192]

Family tradition maintains that the Americans fired arrows from their rifles and muskets, while other accounts state that one of the Americans tossed burning torches onto the home.[193]

The Loyalists tried to knock off the burning shingles, at which point the American artillery opened up on them. Pinned down in a burning house, McPherson raised a white flag and surrendered.[194]

Rebecca's generosity did not end there. She prepared a "sumptuous dinner" for both the American and Loyalist officers. Lee can be trusted, as he was an eyewitness to the events, yet his accounts were written many years later and with clear purpose. Archaeologists working at the site in 2006 found the main plantation home, the British defenses and moat and the site of her secondary home, thus matching Lee's account that "opposite to Fort Motte, to the north, stood another hill, where Mrs. Motte, having been dismissed from her mansion, resided, in the old farm house. On this height Lieutenant Colonel Lee with his corps took post."[195]

Lee worked on his memoirs from 1809 to 1810, and published them in 1812. Heavily in debt, he saw his memoirs as a chance not only to improve his income, but enhance his name and reputation as well.[196] Two of his sons—Henry and Confederate General Robert E. Lee—further edited his memoirs in 1827 and 1869, respectively. Thus the events were repeated from their father's memory and the dialogue may not include the precise words and phrases.[197]

The senior Lee was a good writer whose command of language enabled him to write a work that was popular and appealing. How much he exaggerated or modified events remains unknown, as does the quality of his memory thirty years after the fact. Interestingly enough, Elizabeth Ellet copied Lee's account, almost verbatim, in her work published in 1849.[198]

While traveling through the state to visit Revolutionary War sites in 1849, writer Benson Lossing passed near the site of Fort Motte. Lossing recorded his story based on Lee's writings, as well as other contemporaries and local traditions. He wrote,

To communicate fire to the mansion was Lee's expedient. That officer had enjoyed the hospitality of Mrs. Motte during the siege, and her only marriageable daughter was then the wife of his friend, Major Thomas Pinckney. These circumstances made it a painful duty for him to propose the destruction of her property. Her cheerful acquiescence, and even patriotic desire to be able to serve her country but such a sacrifice, gave him joy and, communicating his plan to Marion, they hastened to execute it. It was proposed to hurl ignited combustibles upon the roof of the house, by arrows. These were prepared, when Mrs. Motte, observing their inferiority, brought out a fine bow and a bundle of arrows which had been brought from the East Indies, and presented them to Lee. On the morning of May 12, 1781, Lee sent Dr. Irvine, of his cavalry, with a flag, to state truly the relative position of the belligerents; that Rawdon had not yet crossed the Santee, and that immediate surrender would save many lives. McPherson still refused compliance and at meridian, when the ditch was advanced within bow shot of the fort, several arrows from the hand of Nathan Savage, a private in Marion's brigade, winged their way, with lighted torches, toward the house. Two struck the dry shingles, and instantly a bright flame crept along the roof. Soldiers were ordered to knock off the shingles and put the fire out, when one or two shots from Marion's battery, raking the loft, drove them below. McPherson hung out a white flag, the firing ceased, the flames were extinguished, and at one o'clock the garrison surrendered themselves prisoners of war. By invitation of Mrs. Motte, both the victorious and the captive officers partook of a scrumptious dinner from her table, while she presided with all the coolness and easy politeness for which she was remarkable when surrounded by friends in the enjoyment of peace.[199]

When Lossing visited the site, he stopped at the home built on the site of Mrs. Motte's house. While there, he could clearly see the Americans' trenches, now slowly filling in from erosion, and damaged trees from the small arms and artillery. He spoke to the property's current owner, as well as local residents, some of whom had known her and were even at the siege.[200]

Rebecca Motte had not seen the last of the war after the soldiers departed her home. In November 1781, a detachment of six dragoons and an officer were sent to protect Mrs. Motte and her daughter. Their mission "with a flag and a few armed men, is to protect the above Ladies from skulking parties, who rob without distinction all they meet."[201]

Ninety Six, South Carolina

Following the battle at Guilford Courthouse, Greene moved his army back into South Carolina to attack various British forts and garrisons. Prior to the battle of Hobkirk's Hill, near Camden, South Carolina, Greene gave orders to the army on April 18, 1781, that women with children and those unable to march must be sent off and not accompany the army. He specifically ordered that "none will be admitted to ride on Waggons or horses, on any pretence whatsoever."[202]

Enforcement of this command must have been a serious problem, for he repeated those orders on March 21, 1782, and again on July 6, 1782, writing, "The wagon master will take care that the wagons are not loaded with women." Washington had the same problem, writing in 1778 from Valley Forge that "the indulgence of suffering Women to ride in Waggons having degenerated into a great abuse, and complaint having been made by the Officers of the day that the Plea of leave from Officers is constantly urged when the Waggon Master rode such Women down: It is expressly ordered that no Officer grant such a leave for the future…is determined in Case a Violation should happen that it shall not pass unnoticed."[203]

After fighting at Hobkirk's Hill in April, General Nathanael Greene moved his army of militia and Continental troops to the British outpost of Ninety Six. This was an important fort in the chain of British posts that controlled the interior of the state. At Ninety Six there was a small village with a jail, courthouse, spring and several houses. The post was at a crossroads, and the entire village had been enclosed with a wall of upright logs, surrounded by a ditch. A large star-shaped earthen fort was added to the north for more protection. The defenders consisted of over one thousand Loyalists under Lieutenant Colonel John Harris Cruger. A large number of civilian refugees had also fled into the fortified town. (How the town got its unusual name has been debated; one theory suggests that it was the estimated distance traders journeyed from there to the Cherokee villages to the west, and another claims that roads crossed a nearby stream six and nine times.)[204]

Upon the approach of Greene's army, he learned that Cruger's wife was staying at the nearby Mayson plantation. Hearing that the Americans were approaching, Mrs. Cruger began to sew her money into her clothing to hide it, fearing the worst. During the month-long siege, she enjoyed pleasant treatment from the Americans. Greene sent an officer to ask whether she wished to stay there or be escorted into the town to join her husband. She replied that she desired to stay at the Mayson home, and Greene sent a twelve-man guard to protect her during the siege operations.[205]

Others were not so fortunate. Mary Horsy, a small farmer who lived nearby, suffered as her property was plundered by the Americans. Her son was killed during the siege, and her husband also died before the close of the war. Mary left with the British forces after the siege and ended up a refugee in Charleston. From there her fate is unknown; she may have evacuated with other refugees when the British abandoned the city at the end of the war.[206]

In the meantime, the Americans began to surround Ninety Six, dig trenches and place artillery. Cruger wrote to his superior, Lord Rawdon, that over one hundred "old and helpless with their families" had sought shelter in the fort. These were women who were either town residents or had accompanied their husbands in the Loyalist militia. These extra persons were not only a strain on his limited food and water resources, but they also crowded an already cramped area and put the garrison at greater risk for disease.[207]

One of the civilians we know of by name was Jane Henderson, a widow and native of Ireland. She had lived in Pennsylvania and later moved to South Carolina. She was nearly seventy years old at the time the town was surrounded and attacked. She evacuated with the British troops to Charleston, where she met up with her son David, her daughter and her two grandchildren. Eventually she moved to Nova Scotia, having lost all her South Carolina property. This information comes from her claim for damages filed with the British government after the war.[208]

Unable to attack directly, Greene's army began a siege. The Americans cut off the town from the outside, blockading the roads, and began digging trenches toward the fort and village. As their artillery was placed, they could bombard the town. With a limited supply of food, water and supplies, the garrison could not hold out long.

Women like Jane Henderson would have spent their time in the few buildings of the town. It was too dangerous to go outside, as the fort was subject to rifle fire from the Americans. Accounts of the action make note of the heat, and conditions would have been difficult, given the inability to move freely, lack of water and limited food supply. For nearly one full month, the garrison struggled in the heat, with little shade and limited water supply.

It was during the siege of Ninety Six that a famous incident involving two women took place. The exploits of Grace and Rachel Martin, two sisters who disguised themselves as men to stop a British messenger, is a well-known local story. The sisters lived near Ninety Six and intercepted the courier during the siege in May of 1781.[209]

Grace and Rachel Martin lived near Ninety Six with their husbands, who were out with the militia. The two women learned that a British messenger was to pass by their houses one evening. Donning their husbands' clothing and with weapons in hand, the two women stopped the messenger, taking his packet and his horse. Local tradition also maintains that the dejected messenger walked back down the road, stopping at one of their houses where the two women, back in their own clothes, fed him.[210]

Meanwhile, back at Ninety Six, for several weeks, the Americans had been digging closer to the Loyalist fortifications. Cut off from supply or reinforcement, the garrison under Cruger was becoming desperate for food and supplies, most importantly fresh water. The large numbers of soldiers and refugees in the town put a strain on the limited supplies.

One interesting incident occurred behind the American lines, yet details are few. On May 30, five wagons arrived from Augusta, Georgia, with supplies. Upon inspecting the contents, an officer found two African American girls. He estimated the ages of the sisters, "from appearance," at eight and six.[211]

None of the wagon drivers knew of their presence, and the girls did not know where they had come from, nor could they describe where they lived. The officer noted, "They told me their Masters name was Johnston and that the said Waggoners came to their Mr's [master's] House & brought them off."[212]

Nothing more is known about the girls; records are silent on what became of them. This is an example of civilians caught up in the movements of armies. Throughout the countryside, civilians were uprooted and became refugees. Perhaps the girls saw a chance to escape, or maybe the wagon drivers took them and lied to the officer; either way, it is a fascinating episode and one that makes us wish to know more.

Ninety Six Village Site. The blue posts mark the corners of the town of Ninety Six. Here stood about a dozen wooden buildings. In the fortified town Loyalist refugees and camp followers sought shelter during the month-long siege. *Photo by author.*

In the meantime, the siege dragged on under a scorching summer sun. At that point, the actions of a local woman helped shape the outcome of the siege. Three British regiments had landed in Charleston and were marching inland to relieve the garrison. Greene knew of their arrival, and was pushing his men hard to finish their preparations for the assault. The garrison, cut off from the outside, was unaware that reinforcements were on the way. There are several versions of the story, each of which will be told here.

One version maintains that Kate Fowler was a local resident who was engaged to a Loyalist officer in the fort. Upon hearing the news that reinforcements were coming, she arranged for a man to inform the garrison. Local civilians often came to the American camp, some out of curiosity, others to sell produce and supplies. One day a lone man in a wagon rode through the camp and slowly on toward the siege lines. Suddenly he cracked his whip and raced past the American guards, headed for the fort's gate. The Loyalist soldiers inside admitted him, and he informed Cruger that help was on the way.[213]

The other version states that Kate Fowler herself was the one who rode into the American camp, made her way up to the front lines and made a break for the fort. This seems less likely, as contemporary writers identify Hugh Aiken as the one who delivered the message. Either way, Cruger's forces now knew that if they held out just a little longer, they would be relieved.[214]

Greene was now forced to change his plans. At first he chose to abandon the siege, but his officers protested and urged an attack. At noon on June 12, the American infantry assaulted the fortified post from two sides. While one group captured their objective, the main attack stalled, suffering roughly 50 percent casualties. The next day Greene retreated, and the following day the fresh British regiments arrived, much to the relief of the garrison.

And what of Kate Fowler? Again, there is no hard evidence. One story says that she was abandoned by her fiancé when the British retreated and burned Ninety Six. Today there is a Kate Fowler Street in the town of Ninety Six, not far from the fort.

Another local woman served the British as well. David Tennant was a sergeant with the South Carolina Royalists, a Loyalist militia. His wife carried dispatches for the British. After the war, the couple returned to Ireland, from where they had emigrated. Being on the losing side, she does not get the attention of an Emily Geiger or Rebecca Motte. Unfortunately, her name has not been recorded in documents.[215]

The British forces evacuated the post at Ninety Six, as it was too isolated to be easily supplied and reinforced from Charleston. On their march back to the coast, many refugees joined the troops. Some were wives and families of Loyalist militiamen who had cast their lot with the British.

General Andrew Pickens wrote that as his forces pursued Cruger's column, they picked up "British prisoners, some Tories, & a number of Families." He also noted "the old Men, Women, & Children we pass'd on to the British lines." Hundreds of women were on their own, husbands were away with the British forces or were dead and these women had to flee, having lost their property.[216]

Alston House, North Carolina
(House in the Horseshoe)

July 29, 1781

In central North Carolina, a small battle occurred at the Alston House, also known as the House in the Horseshoe, since it sits on high ground in a bend of the Deep River in Moore County. Loyalists under Colonel David Fanning had been active in the area. Fanning was a successful and enterprising leader who led raids throughout the area during the war.

Phillip Alston was a wealthy planter and local Whig militia commander. The date of the battle has been disputed by historians; it occurred either on July 29, or August 5 or 6, 1781. Colonel Alston and about twenty men were resting at his house after killing a friend of Fanning a few days before. The home was a two-story wood-framed structure with a front and rear porch. At daybreak, Fanning led a force of about thirty men to attack and take revenge for the earlier incident.[217]

The Loyalists approached and surprised the guards in front of the home; the guards were taken prisoner. Fanning's men opened fire on other soldiers at the gate to the house. The Americans quickly took shelter in the home, with soldiers defending from the windows, doors and porch rails. In the home was Colonel Alston's wife Temperance, who put her two children in the brick fireplace for safety. By having them stand on a table set in the fireplace, they were entirely enclosed by the bricks. She hid in the bed, while musket balls came through the windows of both sides of the house and hit the ceiling above her.[218]

Fanning's troops took cover behind a rail fence that surrounded the home, and the fighting raged for several hours. A British officer—known only as Lieutenant McKay—serving with the Loyalists now led a rush on the house. He no sooner jumped the fence to lead the charge than he was

House in the Horseshoe. Loyalists under Colonel David Fanning surrounded American troops under Colonel Phillip Alston in the home. Bullet holes are still visible in the walls. Here on the porch, Fanning met Temperance Alston and negotiated a truce. *Photo by author*.

shot and killed. Several others who were in the process of straddling the fence were also wounded.[219]

Unable to subdue the defenders, the Loyalists tried to force them out by setting the home on fire. Fanning had a free black man who was with his group try to approach the house unseen and set it on fire. Alston himself saw this unfold and shot and wounded the man before he could accomplish it.

Fanning would not give up so easily, and this time loaded a cart or wagon with straw to set on fire and drive it up to the home. Colonel Alston knew that the wagon would shelter the attackers as they drove it forward, and his wooden house would be engulfed if they succeeded. At that point, Temperance stepped forward to intervene. She suggested she could talk to Fanning to stop the attack. The men, especially her husband, felt it was too dangerous, but she insisted.

She opened the front door, raised a white flag and went out onto the steps. Fanning saw her and called to her to meet him halfway outside. When he came up to her, she said, "We will surrender, sir, on condition that no one shall be injured or otherwise we will make the best defense we can, and if need be, sell our lives as dearly as possible." Fanning, according to historian Eli Caruthers, was so impressed by her courage that he agreed, and the Americans were paroled on the spot.[220]

Alston House, North Carolina (House in the Horseshoe)

Fanning himself described the event in his writings:

> *I...got intelligence that Col. Alstine* [sic] *lying on the banks of Deep River with a party of twenty-five men. We marched all that day and night following, and just as the day dawned we advanced in three divisions up to a house they had thrown themselves into. On our approach we fired upon the house, as I was determined to make examples of them, for behaving in the manner they had done to one of my pilots, by name Kenneth Black. They returned our fire, and the action continued upwards of three hours, when after killing four of them and wounding all the rest, expect three, they sent out a flag to surrender, Col. Astline's lady begging their lives; and on her solicitation I concluded to grant her request.*[221]

Fanning's account mentions more Whig casualties than most other versions, and also places him clearly in control of the situation. He has Temperance "begging" for their lives and decides to "grant her request." At any rate, this is one of the few eyewitness accounts of the action, though it was written many years later. Fanning admits to six casualties in his writings.[222]

General John Butler, commanding nearby Whig militia, wrote of the affair, "Captain Fanning attacked Col. Alston in his own house on Deep River, near the Iron Works. Alston who had between 15 and 20 men and being surprised took refuge in the House, which was only of slabboards; after some firing was obliged to surrender prisoners of War. He had seven Men wounded and Fanning had one or two killed." Butler was not in the battle, but no doubt heard about it from Alston and others. Unfortunately, and strangely, this account makes no mention of Temperance's actions, which were uncommon events that would have stood out to contemporaries.[223]

Writing in the 1800s, Eli Caruthers received his information from local informants, including one defender of the house, and others who knew participants. Several local historians have written about the battle, but accounts differ as to numbers engaged and casualties. Yet most accounts agree on the basic facts. The raid on the house and Temperance's intervention became a local legend. Some of the local stories surrounding the event, especially those recorded later in the 1800s, seem more exaggerated and biased against Fanning; this is not surprising, given the brutal nature of the civil war in this region.[224]

We know very little about Temperance Alston, as she is largely absent from historical documents. She died in either 1788 or 1789, and was

Temperance Alston confronts Colonel David Fanning, negotiating a cease-fire. *Photo by Karen A. Smith.*

Image-only page with header title.

Header title.
Alston House, North Carolina (House in the Horseshoe)

estimated to be in her mid-forties, making her around thirty-five years old at the time of the attack. Like many plantation wives, she was adept at managing the farm and assisting her husband with manual labor, as well as overseeing their finances. She enters the historical record briefly for one moment during battle, and otherwise is a hidden figure.[225]

Eutaw Springs, South Carolina

September 8, 1781

Following the unsuccessful siege of Ninety Six in the backcountry of South Carolina, General Greene turned his attention to the British army that now had retreated to the Congaree River. Led by Lieutenant Colonel Alexander Stewart, the small British force was in a position to watch Greene and defend Charleston.

Greene wrote from Camden in August 1781 that "a Sufficient number of Women, particularly those that have Children must be left as Nurses." The army was preparing to move out toward Eutaw Springs, and no doubt this order intended to limit the women's impact on the army's march.[226]

A hurricane had come through the area in early September, soaking central South Carolina. Swamps and low-lying areas became flooded, necessitating a long, circuitous march by Greene's army. The heavy rains and high winds made life uncomfortable for the troops and followers of the army.

Reinforced by new recruits and anxious to offer battle again, Greene marched against Stewart, who had fallen back to Eutaw Springs. The battle fought there on September 8, 1781, was one of the bloodiest of the war. Greene's forces attacked and caught the British off guard. After several hours of inconclusive fighting, the Americans managed to push the British back and overrun their camp. A counterattack by Loyalist and British forces drove the Americans back, ending the battle.

Attached to Greene's army were no doubt many camp followers, most of whom had probably also been at Cowpens, Camden, Guilford Courthouse and other battles. In addition to the Virginia, Maryland and Delaware troops who had fought together for some time, Greene had been joined by newly raised North Carolina Continental troops. There were also several militia groups that fought here.

Eutaw Springs Battlefield Park. The site today includes two graves, monuments and markers. This was the site of the British camp that was overrun by the Americans. *Photo by author.*

A roster for Captain John Irwin's South Carolina militia company indicates thirty-eight women and eighty-one children were present with his unit in 1781. Most of the women were wives of soldiers, or widows. With nowhere else to go, many widows stayed with the army, as it was a means of support.[227]

Greene had ordered his army's women to remain behind with the sick and wounded at Camden while the troops moved on to Eutaw Springs. Before leaving his camp at the High Hills of Santee, he wrote, "Women, particularly those that have Children must be left as Nurses." It is probable that some would have still accompanied the army on its march. Just before battle, Greene most likely would have left his army's wagons and heavy baggage (along with any women who had come that far), at his last campsite, Burdell's plantation, roughly eight miles from the battlefield. He mentions taking only two wagons as ambulances with him the morning of the battle.[228]

On the British side, Lieutenant Colonel Stewart had several slaves with him, which was not uncommon for British officers. Records indicate that Peggy Fenwick and Jenny Burton were personal servants of Stewart.

British Camp at Eutaw Springs. This is what the British camp may have looked like at Eutaw Springs. During the course of the battle, the British and Loyalist troops were driven back through the camp, and the Americans briefly occupied it. The British then counterattacked and regained the camp. The army's camp followers fled down the road to Charleston during the attack. *Photo by author.*

Fenwick was a seventeen-year-old runaway from Charleston, and Burton was a former slave from Savannah.[229]

There may have been other women with the British baggage: servants, wives of soldiers attached to the army, Loyalist refugees, etc. During the engagement the camp was overrun, and no doubt panic spread among those attached to the army as they fled farther into the rear for safety. Stewart and other British officers rallied their men, counterattacked and drove the Americans back. At that point, with both sides exhausted, the battle ended.

Accounts mention that the day was extremely hot, and the action lasted about four hours (an extremely long time for a battle). Both sides were fatigued by the time the fighting ended. The next day, Stewart buried his dead and began to march back to Charleston. While Greene had not won the battle, he had driven the British from the state's interior, and they now only held the coast.

Thus at Eutaw Springs there were probably few, if any, women with the attacking Americans. They likely would have remained behind that morning. No doubt many women in the British camp were caught up in the panic as their troops retreated and the camp was overrun.

Lindley's Mill, North Carolina

September 13, 1781

Just a few days after the battle at Eutaw Springs, on September 12, Loyalists scored an impressive victory in North Carolina. Led by Colonel David Fanning, a group of Loyalist militia raided the state capital at Hillsboro. They captured supplies, about two hundred soldiers and the governor's council, but more importantly, they took the governor himself—Thomas Burke—captive.[230]

Flush with victory, the Loyalist army began marching their prisoners southeast toward Wilmington, a British stronghold. The next day, on September 13, near Lindley's Mill in Chatham County, local militia tried to stop Fanning and rescue the governor.

American militia attacked the Loyalists as they descended a curve in the road and crossed a stream. Initially, the Loyalists were thrown into confusion and took heavy casualties; however, Fanning managed to counterattack and drive the Americans off. While the Americans attacked the head of the column, another group struck the rear of the Loyalists in an attempt to rescue the prisoners. Under the leadership of Fanning and other officers, this desperate assault was beaten off.[231]

The Loyalist army managed to continue its march toward Wilmington. On a subsequent evening, Governor Burke and several other important prisoners stayed in the home owned by the McRea family. The son of the couple told Caruthers,

> *The Governor was put into an additional apartment at the end of the house, and there closely guarded. Our bag of meal was seized and cooked immediately; and having been previously robbed, my mother had no bed clothes except one cotton sheet which was carefully wrapped round my infant brother John, by his mother's side. One of the company*

seized hold of the corner of this sheet and continued to jerk and shake it until the infant rolled out on the naked floor.[232]

Mrs. McRea's maiden name was Burke, and she hoped to help him escape (though they were probably not related—as she stated, she just wanted revenge on the Loyalists). The informant told Caruthers, "By way of retaliation, my mother made some attempt before day to let her namesake, the Governor, escape, but without success." How she tried to free him and how the guards prevented it is unfortunately not recorded.[233]

Fanning's army was able to deliver his prisoners, including Governor Burke, to British-held Wilmington in one of the most successful Loyalist raids of the entire conflict in the South.

Southeastern North Carolina

Spring 1781

Following the battle at Guilford Courthouse, Cornwallis moved his battered army toward the coast, hoping to resupply. The British had lost one fourth of their strength in this hard-fought battle, but had very little to show for it. At the end of the day they held the ground, but were too weak to pursue Greene or permanently control the region.

Through late March the army moved southeast, intending to resupply at Cross Creek (modern-day Fayetteville). The British forces in Wilmington, however, were unable to penetrate that far to meet them. When Cornwallis reached Cross Creek, he was dismayed that no supplies or reinforcements were waiting for him. Thus he had to move farther east, to the coast itself, to refit his army. The British arrived in Wilmington on April 9.

Observers noted the condition of the battered forces: men were without shoes, they had few wagons and their horses were lean and hungry. The troops were weary from months of active campaigning and hard fighting. Since January, they had been constantly on the move. The women of the army shared in these hardships.

One North Carolina militiaman wrote, "The outrages were committed mostly by a train of loyal refugees." Civilians who had come out to support the British were forced to flee with them when Cornwallis left the vicinity; otherwise they faced revenge from their neighbors. More specifically, he said that the women camp followers were "a swarm of beings (not better than harpies). These were women who followed the army in the character of officer's and soldiers' wives. They were generally mounted on the best horses and side saddles, dressed in the finest and best clothes that could be taken from the inhabitants." Despite British efforts to control the plundering by their women since February and March, apparently the problem continued.[234]

Many runaway slaves joined the British army during their march across the Carolinas. *Photo by Karen A. Smith.*

Refugee Janet Murchison shared in the British army's odyssey across the state. Her husband John had been captured at Moores Creek in 1776 and imprisoned in Philadelphia. Upon release, he managed to join the British forces when they invaded South Carolina in 1780.

Janet rejoined him here, but he died of wounds following the Battle of Camden in August. Alone and in hostile territory, Janet accompanied the army through the fall and winter, arriving at Wilmington the following April. Sick and unable to travel, she remained in the port city when Cornwallis's army left for Virginia. She lost all the property that she and her husband owned in Anson and Cumberland Counties.[235]

After remaining in Wilmington for a few weeks, the British left, marching north. Through the spring and summer, Cornwallis's army moved across eastern North Carolina and into Virginia. By the fall, they had moved down the Virginia Peninsula toward Williamsburg and Jamestown. At Yorktown, the British and German troops dug in, expecting resupply and reinforcement from British-held New York. Before that could happen, General Washington's main army, joined by French forces, surrounded Cornwallis.

Yorktown was one of the largest military operations of the war, and involved land and naval forces of both sides. The Continental army, Virginia militia, a French expeditionary force, British and German troops were all present for the two-week siege. One brief example of a woman in the trenches is Sarah Osborn, wife of Sergeant Aaron Osborn of the Third New York Regiment of Washington's army. She cooked food and brought it to the men in the trenches during the bombardment, and was even in the trenches on the day Cornwallis surrendered.[236]

That fall and winter, the armies in the Carolinas settled into a stalemate, as both sides knew negotiations were underway to end the war. This did not stop the roaming bands of guerillas, who continued to raid and harass their enemies among the civilian population. For the common people of the Carolinas, the bitter civil war continued into a new year as 1782 approached.

General Thomas Sumter wrote in December 1781, "The Number and Retchedness of the Women & Children Cant be Conceived. Utterly out of the power of Many to Move, or Subsist Much longer where they are."[237]

Bacon's Bridge, South Carolina

Summer 1782

While major fighting ended in the early fall of 1781, the armies still launched raids throughout the winter and into the summer of 1782. British forces, severely weakened after Eutaw Springs, held only Charleston, and launched raids into the interior for supplies. Greene moved his army close to the city to watch for opportunities to strike. He had been reinforced with troops from Washington's army after the victory at Yorktown the previous fall. Both sides knew that peace negotiations were underway and that the war was winding down. That spring the American army of General Greene was camped near Bacon's Bridge, near Dorchester, about twenty miles north of Charleston.

On March 5, 1782, Greene's orders for the day noted that two soldiers from the Second Maryland Regiment, John Young and Patrick Noling, along with their wives Mary Young and Elizabeth Noling, were tried for "receiving and concealing stolen goods." Patrick was found innocent, John was to receive one hundred lashes, and Mary and Elizabeth were to be "Drumd out of the Army and never to return." This is an excellent example of women being subject to military discipline like their husband soldiers.[238] A week later, the women were allowed to return, apparently at the request of officers of the regiment. Greene noted, however, that they may "rejoin, but their stay will depend on their future good behaviour."[239]

Despite being so close to victory, discontent was widespread in the American ranks. Years of inconsistent pay and poor rations were taking their toll on the men. In the spring of 1782, Sergeant Richard Peters of Maryland was recruited by British spies to "corrupt" the soldiers in his command. Peters was to get his fellow officers to mutiny, and march the men who were willing to follow them out to a designated place, where they would meet up with British troops.[240]

A camp follower sewing in camp. *Photo by Karen A. Smith.*

A sergeant's wife named Becky overheard the plot one evening and reported it the next morning. Greene ordered General Mordecai Gist of Maryland to "take Down in writing the Substance of Becky's evidence against Gosnell etc." Peters was convicted and hanged, and Sergeant Gosnell (or Gornell) of Pennsylvania was tried and shot on April 22. The mutiny never got off the ground due to this swift reaction by Greene.[241]

Several other officers involved with the plot were arrested and sent to a rear area. An order states that five officers and men of Pennsylvania and Maryland "with their wives and families" were to be sent to Salisbury, North Carolina, to be employed in repairing equipment and supplies. Unfortunately, records do not name Becky's husband or provide her last name.[242]

Women with Greene's army in the Carolinas provided a number of common services, and a letter written in June of 1782 reveals one of them. Greene's papers state that "the women of the Army have lately sold large quantities of tallow" that they received at the slaughter pen. The tallow was used for making soap.[243]

Conclusion

It seems clear that women were in most, if not all, of the battles in the Southern Campaign. They traveled with the armies as camp followers, or visited the battlefields to nurse the wounded and search for relatives. Both the British and American regular armies each had their camp followers—those women attached to the regiments who worked and received pay and rations. In the bloody and bitter militia struggle, women were caught up in the civil war that raged among neighbors and communities. Some are in fact buried on the various battlefields.

While these women were undoubtedly there, they are hard to find. Women were probably so common that writers, who were mostly men, did not take notice of them. They were part of the army, part of the camp and part of the experience. Like horses and wagons, women were present but often not specifically mentioned.

Surprisingly enough, they often had important, though little appreciated, impacts on events, as at Ninety Six, Cowpens, Fishing Creek and Kings Mountain. It is hoped through this research that we will gain a fuller understanding of the War for Independence and the people involved with it. It is also the intention of this work to identify as fully as possible these women and sort myth from reality.

One interesting observation made by historian Todd Braisted is that as the war progressed, the number of men in a unit generally declined, but the number of women often remained the same. Battle deaths, desertion, disease and transfer account for this: in active campaigning, a unit's combat strength naturally goes down. Women, not generally exposed to battle and not subject to transfer or assignment like soldiers, would have remained with the unit.[244]

Conclusion

The presence of women on these battlefields is important to note, as it fills a gap in our understanding of these events. Historian Stephanie G. Wolf wrote, "The center stage of history has always been occupied by great events…the daily lives of…people, from the stars to the bit players to the walk-ons, formed the real web of the eighteenth century." To understand the real war, and the reality of these events, we must know these people.[245]

Preserving the Past

Many of the battle sites where women were present are preserved today. The following list, in chronological order, describes how to visit these sites.

MOORES CREEK

MOORES CREEK NATIONAL BATTLEFIELD
40 Patriots Hall Drive
Currie, NC 28435
910.283.5591
www.nps.gov/mocr
While there were probably no women at the battle of Moores Creek, the park does have a monument honoring women in the Revolution. In front of the monument are the graves of Mary Slocumb and her husband Ezekiel. Their remains were moved to the site in the 1920s. The site is located about twenty miles from Wilmington, North Carolina.

MUSEUM OF THE CAPE FEAR HISTORICAL COMPLEX
801 Arsenal Avenue
Fayetteville, NC 28305
910.486.1300
http://ncmuseumofhistory.org/osm/mcf.html
Also in downtown Fayetteville, a historic marker stands on Cool Springs Street, noting where Flora MacDonald watched the army assemble.

BARBECUE PRESBYTERIAN CHURCH
124 Barbecue Church Road
Sanford, NC 27332

919.499.5211
Flora MacDonald worshiped here and lived nearby. A marker denotes the site of the original church, and the old spring used in the colonial period still flows.

SAVANNAH

SAVANNAH HISTORY MUSEUM
303 Martin Luther King Jr. Boulevard
Savannah, GA 31401
www.chsgeorgia.org
This museum has exhibits on the siege of Savannah. Many women were with the garrison in the town, as well as with the besieging American and French forces. The museum reconstructed the Spring Hill Redoubt in 2005, focal point of the American and French attack that failed. The site had been covered by facilities of the Georgia Railroad. The redoubt site is still being developed, but the museum plans to focus more on the Revolutionary events in Savannah.

CHARLESTON

CHARLESTON MUSEUM
360 Meeting Street
Charleston, SC 29403
843.722.2996
www.ego.net/us/sc/chs/cmuseum
This museum documents the history of the city, including the siege of 1780. Nearby in Marion Square is the only remaining section of the Revolutionary defenses that surrounded the city. This tabby (mortar and shell) wall extended across the front of the city, and its location serves to illustrate the size of the colonial city.

WILLIAMSON'S PLANTATION

HISTORIC BRATTONSVILLE
1444 Brattonsville Road
McConnells, SC 29726
803.684.2327
www.chmuseums.org/ourmuseums/hb
The Bratton House stands here amid a living history farm. In 2007, Brattonsville announced that archaeologists had found the location of the Williamson house, where the attack occurred. The historic site is located about ten miles south of York, South Carolina, off U.S. 321.

Hanging Rock

The Hanging Rock battlefield is privately owned; there is no public access to the areas of fighting. The intersection of Flat Rock Road (SC 15) and Hanging Rock Road, just a few miles below Heath Springs, is the center of the battlefield. A historic marker here notes the Ingram House, center of the British camp, and where George Washington spent the night during his presidential tour.

Several nearby historic sites discuss the battle and the Jackson family's involvement:
MUSEUM OF THE WAXHAWS
PO Box 7
Waxhaw, NC 28173
704.843.1832
www.perigee.net/~mwaxhaw

ANDREW JACKSON STATE PARK
196 Andrew Jackson Park Road
Lancaster, SC 29720
803.285.3344
www.southcarolinaparks.com/park-finder/state-park/1797.aspx

WAXHAW PRESBYTERIAN CHURCH
2814 Old Hickory Road
Lancaster, SC 29720
The church is the burial site of Andrew Jackson's mother, Elizabeth. A marker stands to her, though her actual gravesite is unknown. The current building is the third to stand on the site. Settlers established the original church in 1750.

Camden

CAMDEN BATTLEFIELD
www.palmettoconservation.org.
The Camden battlefield, currently protected by the State of South Carolina, is open to the public. The battlefield has been recently preserved, and is located about eight miles north of the town on SC Route 15. Taking this road north from the battlefield toward Heath Springs (and Hanging Rock) follows the route of the American retreat, where many camp followers were caught up with the fleeing army.

FISHING CREEK

Most of the Fishing Creek Battlefield has been inundated by the flooding of the Catawba River. The site lies north of Great Falls, along U.S. 21. A state historical marker stands near the site of the battle.

STALLIONS

The Stallion house stood off SC Route 5 near York, South Carolina. There is nothing today marking the site where Mrs. Stallion was killed.

KINGS MOUNTAIN

KINGS MOUNTAIN NATIONAL MILITARY PARK
2625 Park Road
Blacksburg, SC 29702
864.936.7921
www.nps.gov/kimo
This park preserves this pivotal 1780 battle site. Ferguson's grave is located along the battlefield trail. While no mention is made of her, Virginia Sal is also buried in the grave with Ferguson. The Loyalist campsite is on top of the ridge, where the eighty-foot-tall U.S. Monument stands. There, on a rainy evening, Virginia Sal spent her last night.

BICKERSTAFF'S PLANTATION

A state historic marker notes the site where nine Loyalist prisoners were hanged a few days after the battle. The wives of some of the prisoners were here with the army, and Mrs. Bickerstaff cut down the bodies and buried them after they were hanged. The marker is located on Whiteside Road, northeast of Rutherfordton, North Carolina.

GILBERT TOWN

Gilbert Town no longer exists, but the site was north of modern Rutherfordton. A state historic marker stands on U.S. 221 north of the town. The site was on Rock Road. Here Ferguson's army camped, and several women were held as prisoners.

OVERMOUNTAIN VICTORY NATIONAL HISTORIC TRAIL

www.nps.gov/ovvi
The trail preserves sections of the route taken by the American army on their march to Kings Mountain, and also provides a driving tour using modern highways. Bickerstaff's Plantation, Gilbert Town and other sites of importance are linked in this program to preserve the story of the march.

COWPENS

COWPENS NATIONAL BATTLEFIELD
PO Box 308
Chesnee, SC 29323
864.461.2828
www.nps.gov/cowp
This battlefield is located north of Interstate 85 in upper South Carolina, near Spartanburg.

WALNUT GROVE PLANTATION
1200 Otts Shoals Road
Roebuck, SC 29376
864.576.6546
Kate Moore Barry, who helped gather the militia the night before the battle of Cowpens, is buried here. It is one of the oldest houses in the area.

GUILFORD COURTHOUSE

GUILFORD COURTHOUSE NATIONAL MILITARY PARK
2331 New Garden Road
Greensboro, NC 27410
336.288.1776
www.nps.gov/guco
This National Park features a monument to women at tour stop #1 near the Visitor Center. The museum also discusses camp followers with the army. The courthouse stood near tour stop #5, and here many wounded would have been treated by the women of the British army.

TANNENBAUM HISTORIC PARK
2200 New Garden Road
Greensboro, NC 27410
336.545.5315
www.greensboro-nc.gov/Departments/Parks/facilities/tannenbaum
This historic site, at the edge of the battlefield, was the site of a farm where wounded were treated after the fighting. The British army's camp followers labored here.

GREENSBORO HISTORICAL MUSEUM
130 Summit Avenue
Greensboro, NC 27401

336.373.2043
www.greensborohistory.org
The museum has the pitchfork used by Jane Alexander in defending her house from a Loyalist raid.

New Garden Meeting House
A state historic marker stands at New Garden Meeting House in Greensboro, at the intersection of New Garden Road and Friendly Avenue. Here British wounded were treated after the battle, and British graves may be seen there today.

Ninety Six

Ninety Six National Historic Site
PO Box 496
Ninety Six, SC 29666
864.543.4068
www.nps.gov/nisi
The site of the village of Ninety Six has been marked at this park. Here civilian refugees crowded into the fortified town during the 1781 siege.

Fort Motte

Located along the south bank of the Congaree River in Calhoun County, the site is privately owned and currently inaccessible. Archaeologists discovered the remains of the fort and mansion, as well as Rebecca Motte's outbuilding, in 2006.

Alston House

House in the Horseshoe State Historic Site
288 Alston House Road
Sanford, NC 27330
910.947.2051
www.ah.dcr.state.nc.us/sections/hs/horsesho/PALSTON.HTML
Visitors can still see bullet holes in the house from the 1781 battle that raged here. In front of the house, Temperance Alston met Colonel David Fanning to negotiate the surrender of the house's defenders.

Eutaw Springs

Eutaw Springs Battlefield Park
This roadside park, on SC 9 just east of Eutawville, has no visitor facilities. The park preserves a section of the British campsite that was overrun by the Americans. Heavy fighting raged in the area covered by the park and

the surrounding private property. The British army's camp followers and Loyalist refugees fled in terror down the road toward Charleston when the Americans broke through and entered the camp (following modern SC 9 to the east).

LINDLEY'S MILL

A marker for the Lindley's Mill battlefield is located along Lindley's Mill Road in Alamance County. During the fighting, Governor Burke was held in the Springs Friends Meeting. A modern meetinghouse stands here now; the site is nearby on the Greensboro–Chapel Hill Road. Both locations are accessible from NC 87, south of Burlington.

SOUTHEASTERN NORTH CAROLINA

The British march from Cross Creek (modern Fayetteville) to Wilmington generally followed modern NC 87. The army occupied Wilmington for three weeks in April of 1781, camped within the area bounded by modern Fifth, Orange and Castle Streets. Among the roughly two thousand British troops were several camp followers and Loyalist refugees.

CAPE FEAR MUSEUM
814 Market Street
Wilmington, NC 28401
910.798.4350
www.capefearmuseum.com
The Cape Fear Museum discusses the history of Wilmington and has exhibits on the Revolutionary period.

BURGWIN-WRIGHT HOUSE
224 Market Street
Wilmington, NC 28401
910.762.0570
www.burgwinwrighthouse.com
The Burgin-Wright House was General Cornwallis's headquarters when the army occupied the city. The historic home is open for tours.

BACON'S BRIDGE

The site of Bacon's Bridge was on the Ashley River near Summerville, South Carolina. The campsite where a camp follower spoiled an attempted mutiny is inaccessible today.

The following interpretive groups focus on preserving and presenting women's history:

COMMON KNOWLEDGE
www.commonknowledge18c.org
Common Knowledge is a living history group that interprets the lives of women in the Carolina backcountry during the Revolution. These living historians thoroughly research their topics and demonstrate various skills during their presentations. The women discuss medicine, cooking, natural dyeing, spinning and weaving and clothing. Their website contains a wealth of information on these tasks, and they appear at many of the historic sites listed above.

PAST MASTERS
www.pastmasters.info/index.htm
Based in Pennsylvania, the group Past Masters preserves the skills and knowledge of women in the mid-Atlantic colonies. The members have researched and documented their information, focusing on skills like laundry, making soap, natural dyeing, spinning, food ways and agricultural skills. They have also published *The Pennsylvania Housewife*, not only an excellent cookbook but also an indispensable reference on what foods were available in the eighteenth century and how to cook for each season.

Notes

Introduction

1. Norton, "What An Alarming Crisis," in *Southern Experience*, ed. Crow and Tise, 205.

Part I

2. Norton, *Liberty's Daughters*, 13; Fischer, *Suspect Relations*, 100; Berkin, *Revolutionary Mothers*, 10.

3. Wolf, *As Various as Their Land*, 86–87.

4. Watson, "Women in Colonial North America," 4; Spruill, *Women's Life and Work*, 340–41; Kierner, *Beyond the Household*, 23–25. All of these works are excellent sources on the topic of women's legal status.

5. Fischer, *Suspect Relations*, 4.

6. Brown, *Good Wives*, 104.

7. Berkin, *Revolutionary Mothers*, 11.

8. Royster, *Revolutionary People*, 301, 135–36, 295–97. While they were just as dedicated and supportive of their cause as the men, women were subject to disappointment and some encouraged men to desert or not reenlist.

9. Mayer, *Belonging to the Army*, 124, 150–51.

10. Wolf, *As Various as Their Land*, 83.

11. Mayer, *Belonging to the Army*, 8, 126, 155.

12. Ibid., 2. An eighteenth-century army had a high ratio of combatants to support personnel when compared to the modern military. There were vivandieres or cantiniers with the Union and Confederate armies of the Civil War, but there were not many in comparison to the size of the regiment. Most were sent home after 1861, when the romance of war rubbed off and serious fighting began. While a few did accompany their units throughout the war, and many were wounded or killed in action, these females were never in proportion to the women who accompanied a Revolutionary war regiment into action, nor did they perform quite the same support function.

13. Ibid., 1–2; Royster, *Revolutionary People*, 1–6; Martin and Lender, *Respectable Army*, 27, 31.

14. Mayer, *Belonging to the Army*, 7–8.

15. Ibid., 2–4.

16. Rees, "Multitude of Women."

17. DePauw, "Women in Combat," 212; Mayer, *Belonging to the Army*, 138, 155, 255, 258; Berkin, *Revolutionary Mothers*, 51–53, 56. Information varies on whether American

women received half or full rations. There was also variation by state, as each had its own regulations for its troops.

18. Hagist, "Women of the Army."

19. Ibid., 19.

20. Curtis, *British Army*, 10–11; Martin and Lender, *Respectable Army*, 186. Accurate figures are available for many campsites in the Northern theater. For example the American army was ten thousand men strong with one thousand women at Newburgh, New York, at the end of war.

21. Blumenthal, *Women Camp Followers*, 43; Kopperman, "British High Command," 25; Wright, *Notes on the Continental Army*, 63; Tulley, *The Packet II*, 22, 23. For drumming someone out of camp, the troops were lined up and the prisoner brought out in front. The offender wore a sign around his neck with the offense written on it while a drummer led him. Drummers also marched behind, all beating the Rogue's March. Upon reaching the end of camp, the prisoner was kicked in the rear and sent out. Banishment was a serious threat, especially for someone far from home and with no means of support or protection.

22. Berkin, *Revolutionary Mothers*, 54.

23. Ibid., 51.

24. Mayer, *Belonging to the Army*, 13–14, 17, 137, 138, 218, 233, 275; Berkin, *Revolutionary Mothers*, 51, 57–58, 59. Unlike what is seen in modern reenacting, historically women did not usually cook for the men in camp. Their most common chore was laundry.

25. Kopperman, "British High Command," 32.

26. De Pauw, "Women in Combat," 211.

27. Berkin, *Revolutionary Mothers*, 62.

28. Salley, *Records of Regiments*.

29. Women did serve with each nation that sent troops to fight in North America— French, Spanish and German—but this study focuses primarily on those with the American and British troops.

30. Berkin, *Revolutionary Mothers*, 60; De Pauw, "Women in Combat," 218. While over four hundred women can be documented as serving disguised as males in the Civil War, only a handful are known for the Revolution. Dressing as a man and entering a male realm was socially unacceptable. Of those who did, Deborah Sampson of Massachusetts is the most famous; her story has been well told by historians.

31. Berkin, *Revolutionary Mothers*, 55.

32. Ibid., 59.

33. Ibid., 55.

34. Ibid., 54.

35. Claghorn, *Women Patriots*, 22.

36. Norton, "What an Alarming Crisis," 219.

37. Trussell, *Pennsylvania Line*, 252; Selsky, *Demographic Survey*, 21; Travers, "Were They All Shorter?" These are admittedly very limited samplings, yet comparing men from various regions of America reveals a statistical average for height.

38. Wolf, *As Various as Their Land*, 140.

39. Smith, unpublished research.

40. Ibid. Smith has been researching clothing in the region from primary sources for several years. This borrows on that research, which will be forthcoming. The author is grateful to her for sharing this difficult to find, unpublished data.

41. *Pennsylvania Housewife*, 10, 21.

42. Smith, "What Really Killed Women?;" Sandy Levins, "Was Death by Fire Common?" This last article draws on research, both experimental and archival, done by Dr. Clarissa Dillon.

43. Rees, *Foundation of an Army*, 49-64.

44. Ibid.; Tulley, *The Packet*, 2–3. Of course, the ideal was hardly ever really gotten in the field, and the armies adapted as conditions dictated.

45. Tulley, *The Packet IV*, 34.
46. Ibid., 35.

Part II

47. Dunkerly, *Redcoats on the River*, 116.
48. Ellet, *Women of the Revolution*, 143.
49. MacLeod, *Flora MacDonald*, 4.
50. Lossing, *Reflections of Rebellion*, 70.
51. Ibid. Some historians have questioned the authenticity of this, with understandable misgivings. To his defense, Lossing often exaggerated, but never manufactured his stories.
52. McCrady, *History of South Carolina*, 178–79.
53. Ibid., 169. "Firelocks" refers to the flintlock weapons used at the time.
54. Moore, *The Loyalists*, 80; MacLeod, *Flora MacDonald*, 193. Flora lost ten horses and fifty cattle, as well as plates, books and furniture.
55. MacLeod, *Flora MacDonald*, 17, 213.
56. Moore, *The Loyalists*, 216; Ellet, *Women of the Revolution*, 149; Demond, *Loyalists in North Carolina*, 113, 122, 184; MacLeod, *Flora MacDonald*, 217–18; Caruthers, *Revolutionary Incidents*, 96. Again, her story was exaggerated by writers, claiming that she insisted on staying on deck rather than go below and animated the sailors to fight. No positive date is known for her return, but it seems to have been either 1777 or 1778. There is also a story that two daughters of Flora visited friends in the Black family, and Whig militia stopped them, took their gold rings and their silk handkerchiefs from their necks and split their dresses with swords, stripping them of their outer clothing. It is difficult to ascertain how accurate this is. The story seems to originate in the 1800s with Caruthers, who does not document it.
57. MacLeod, *Flora MacDonald*, 142, 237.
58. Slocumb, Federal Pension Application.
59. Hubbell to Hatch, Office Memorandum.
60. Ibid, 18–20.
61. Maze to Haines.
62. Ellet, *Women of the Revolution*, 305.
63. Blumenthal, *Women Camp Followers*, 93; Ira Gruber, *John Peeble's The American War*, 332; Hagist, "Women of the Army."
64. Curtis, *British Army*, 11.
65. James, *Siege of Savannah*, 63.
66. Ibid.
67. Braisted, "Female Ancestors."
68. James, *Siege of Savannah*, 64.

Part III

69. *Pennsylvania Housewife*, 11, 12; Wolf, *As Various as Their Land*, 93.
70. *Pennsylvania Housewife*, 11, 16–17.
71. Tustin, *Diary of the American War*, 389. The wives of Jaegers were washerwomen.
72. Newsome, "British Orderly Book," 279; Braisted, "Female Ancestors."
73. Frey, *Water From the Rock*, 122–23.
74. Moultrie, *Memoirs*, 62.
75. Ibid., 71.
76. Wilson, *Southern Strategy*, x.
77. Ibid., 248.
78. Borick, *Gallant Defense*, 152–53.
79. Ibid.

80. Ibid.

81. Ibid. Many civilians outside the city suffered. The following list is just a sampling: Mrs. Roddick's shoes were stolen, Widow Broughton had "every thing that belonging to her" taken, Mrs. Butler claimed she lost "every thing" and Eliza Wilkinson wrote that her home was looted, and even the women's caps were pulled off.

82. Scoggins, *Day it Rained Militia*, 69; Ellet, *Women of the Revolution*, vol. 3, 225–26.

83. Scoggins, *Day it Rained Militia*, 70.

84. Ibid., 103.

85. Ibid.

86. Ibid., 104.

87. Ibid., 105.

88. Borick, *Gallant Defense*, 152.

89. *Battle of Huck's Defeat*, 5; Scoggins, *Day it Rained Militia*, 105.

90. *Battle of Huck's Defeat*, 6; Scoggins, *Day it Rained Militia*, 106.

91. Scoggins, *Day it Rained Militia*, 106.

92. Ibid., 107.

93. Ibid.

94. Ibid; *Battle of Huck's Defeat*, 6–7. A local story surfaced in the 1800s that Martha considered poisoning Huck's food, but hesitated at the last moment. The origin of the story, and its accuracy, remain unknown.

95. Scoggins, *Day it Rained Militia*, 107.

96. Ibid., 118.

97. Ibid., 118, 121; *Battle of Huck's Defeat*, 7.

98. Scoggins, *Day it Rained Militia*, 121.

99. Draper, 13 DD 85.

100. Braisted, "Female Ancestors."

101. Booraem, *Young Hickory*, 69.

102. Ellet, *Women of the Revolution*, 168.

103. Ibid., 256–57.

104. Tarleton, *Campaigns of 1780 and 1781*, 246; Wickwire, *Cornwallis*, 59.

105. Ward, *War of the Revolution*, 720; Scheer and Rankin, *Rebels and Redcoats*, 405.

106. Rees, "Number of Rations."

107. Kierner, *Southern Women*, 182.

108. Ward, *War of the Revolution*, 721.

109. Moultrie, *Memoirs*, 236.

110. *Royal Gazette*.

111. Dudley, "Sketch of the Military."

112. Draper, 9 VV 230, 330. Some historians have speculated whether she remained unmarried on purpose or because of her Loyalist sympathies.

113. Saye, *Memoirs of McJunkin*, 17.

114. Draper, 9 VV 317, 14 VV 209, 212. Nothing is mentioned of her husband or children in these records.

115. Ibid., 14 VV 322, 333.

116. Ibid., 14 VV 213.

117. Ibid., 15 VV 311.

118. Ibid., 14 VV 177.

119. Ibid.

120. Ibid.

121. Ibid., 16 VV 55; Gordon, Federal Pension Application; Wallace, Federal Pension Application. Draper often exaggerated, and it is not unlike him to focus on the tragic irony of this story.

122. Draper, 23 VV 232–34.

123. Ibid., 13 VV 178–200.

124. Ibid.

125. Ibid., 16 VV 70–71.
126. Ibid., 13 VV 144.

Part IV

127. *Pennsylvania Housewife*, 11, 12.
128. Newsome, "British Orderly Book," 71.
129. Ibid., 183.
130. Howard and Gerhardt, *Mary Patton*, 1–3.
131. Draper, 6 DD 114, 123, 133, 134.
132. Ibid., 7 DD 17.
133. Moss, *Uzal Johnson*, 62.
134. Ibid.
135. Draper, 4 DD 102.
136. Ibid., 15 DD 44.
137. Ibid., 7 DD 142a. Researcher Karen A. Smith has suggested that their names were not Virginia Sal and Virginia Paul at all, but that perhaps they were two women from Virginia: one named Sally the other Polly.
138. Ibid., 6 DD 42, 153; Black, *First Baptist Church*, 43. Several accounts in Draper and other secondary sources mention that Virginia Sal had red hair. This may have been oral tradition passed down from veterans to family members, who passed it on to informants that wrote to Draper.
139. Black, *First Baptist Church*, 56; Gilchrist, *Patrick Ferguson*, 69; Durham, "Woman Buried With Ferguson"; Robert M. Dunkerly, *Kings Mountain*, 26.
140. Draper, 15 DD 61; 6 DD 13.
141. McQueen, Federal Pension Application.
142. This might explain why the woman described Ferguson to the Americans. Most histories of the battle assume that this woman was Virginia Paul, and that for some reason she told how to identify Ferguson.
143. Collins, *Autobiography*, 53.
144. Draper, 14 DD 65.
145. Black, *First Baptist Church*, 40.
146. Draper, *Kings Mountain*, 306; Claghorn, *Women Patriots*, 134–35.
147. Draper, 6 DD 153, 155.
148. Draper, *Kings Mountain*, 344.
149. Moss, *Uzal Johnson*, 77.

Part V

150. Fagan, *Little Ice Age*, xiii, 100.
151. While many histories estimate the engagement lasted an hour, recent research by Dr. Lawrence Babits suggests it may have only been half an hour, or perhaps even shorter.
152. Conrad, *Papers of Nathanael Greene*, Vol. VIII, 48.
153. Ibid., 26, 133.
154. Tarleton, *Campaigns of 1780 and 1781*, 246. This suggests women did sometimes accompany detachments on such excursions, since he insisted none come on this particular mission.
155. Moss, *Patriots at Cowpens*, 162; Babits, *Devil of a Whipping*, 50–52; Young, *South Carolina Women Patriots*.
156. Moss, *Patriots at Cowpens*, 18; Landrum, *Spartanburg County*, 328; Claghorn, *Women Patriots*, 20; Young, *South Carolina Women Patriots*. Sources indicate that at other times she was a scout for the Whigs and was captured and flogged by the Loyalists. This is a local tradition, and no detailed accounts of such an event could be verified.

157. Claghorn, *Women Patriots*, 20.
158. Graham, *General Daniel Morgan*, 467.
159. Babits, *Devil of a Whipping*, 54, 56.
160. Ibid., 139.
161. Ibid., 134.
162. Ibid., 135.
163. Caruthers, *Revolutionary Incidents*, 211.
164. Ibid., 228.
165. Newsome, "British Orderly Book," 287. It must be remembered that a daily ration of alcohol was not a luxury, but was considered a basic part of a soldier's ration. It was given for stamina and health reasons, and its disappearance was a sign of the desperate state of supplies.
166. Hagist, "Women of the Army."
167. Cornwallis to Rawdon; Stedman, *History of the Origin*, 373–74.
168. Caruthers, *Revolutionary Incidents*, 223.
169. Ibid.
170. Ibid.
171. Ibid., 228.
172. Stedman, *History of the Origin*, 374; Tarleton, *Campaigns of 1780 and 1781*, 270.
173. Black, Federal Pension Application. This information comes from a grandson in the file of Black's pension application; neither Hugh nor Sarah ever mentioned her service in their documents.
174. Claghorn, *Women Patriots*, 193.
175. Conrad, *Papers of Nathanael Greene*, Vol. IX, 69.
176. Lee, *Memoirs of General Henry Lee*, 248.
177. Caruthers, *Revolutionary Incidents*, 230.
178. Ibid., 231.
179. Rees, *Foundation of an Army*.
180. Account of Articles Received at New Garden Meeting House, 179.
181. Kennett, "Killing on Minden Road"; Zachman, e-mail to author.

Part VI

182. Lossing, *Reflections of Rebellion*, 171; Helsley, *South Carolinians*, 65.
183. Lee, *Memoirs of General Henry Lee*, 346; Smith, et. al., *"Obstinate and Strong"*, 14, 21.
184. Smith, et. al., *"Obstinate and Strong,"* 22. The troops were from the British Eighty-fourth Highland Regiment, the Ditfurth or Benning German Regiment and Provincial Loyalists. This was fairly common, even in small garrisons, to have a mix of British, German and Loyalist troops.
185. Ibid., 23.
186. Lee, *Memoirs of General Henry Lee*, 346.
187. Ibid.
188. Ibid., 347.
189. Ibid.
190. Ibid.; Ellet, *Women of the Revolution*, 70.
191. Lee, *Memoirs of General Henry Lee*, 347.
192. Ibid., 348; Ellet, *Women of the Revolution*, 70.
193. Helsley, *South Carolinians*, 66; Smith, et. al., *"Obstinate and Strong,"* 25. Accounts disagree as to whether arrows or a rosin ball were used to burn the house, but arrows shot from a musket seem the most practical and likely method. Examination by archaeologists at the site concludes that the distance was too great for rosin balls to be thrown, and arrows shot from muskets would have worked very well. A grandson of Rebecca also noted that small arms were used.
194. Lee, *Memoirs of General Henry Lee*, 348.

195. Ibid; Smith, et. al., *"Obstinate and Strong,"* 59. What she prepared has not been recorded. Archaeologists discovered the site of her smaller home, as well as the location of the plantation house and its defenses, in 2006. A marker had been on the site since 1909, but the exact location of the home was unknown to the landowners.

196. Lee, *Memoirs of General Henry Lee*, iii, vi.

197. Ibid., viii.

198. Ellet, *Women of the Revolution*, 70–71.

199. Lossing, *Reflections of Rebellion*, 151.

200. Ibid., 148; 47–8.

201. Conrad, *Papers of Nathanael Greene*, Vol. IX, 531.

202. Ibid., Vol. VIII, 111.

203. Ibid., Vol. X, 259; Vol. XI, 398; Blumenthal, *Women Camp Followers*, 74.

204. Jerome Greene, *Historic Resources Study*, 4.

205. Ibid., 123.

206. Moss, *Loyalists at Ninety Six*, 63.

207. Dunkerly and Williams, *Old Ninety Six*, 83.

208. Moss, *Loyalists at Ninety Six*, 59.

209. Ellet, *Women of the Revolution*, 275.

210. Ibid.

211. Greene, *Historic Resources Study*, 135.

212. Ibid.

213. Dunkerly and Williams, *Old Ninety Six*, 42.

214. Latham, *Revolutionary War in the Upcountry*, 153; Dunkerly and Williams, *Old Ninety Six*; Stedman, *History of the Origin*, 415; Lee, *Memoirs of General Henry Lee*, 374; Bass, *Ninety Six*, 398; Moss, *Loyalists at Ninety Six*, 1. It seems that it was definitely Aiken who delivered the message, as several eyewitnesses verify this.

215. Moss, *Loyalists at Ninety Six*, 121.

216. Conrad, *Papers of Nathanael Greene*, Vol. IX, 48.

217. George Wilcox, *House in the Horseshoe*, 178; Thompson and Smith, *House in the Horseshoe*, 11.

218. Caruthers, *Revolutionary Incidents*, 44; Thompson and Smith, *House in the Horseshoe*, 11. It seems strange that she was not under the bed for better protection, but all accounts mention her *in* the bed.

219. Thompson and Smith, *House in the Horseshoe*, 44–45.

220. Ibid., 45.

221. Robinson, *History of Moore County*, 78.

222. Ibid., 78–79. Fanning wrote his account ten years later, after he had relocated to Nova Scotia.

223. Ibid., 79.

224. Thompson and Smith, *House in the Horseshoe*, 12–14; Wellman, *Story of Moore County*, 82; Wilcox, *House in the Horseshoe*, 172. It is not surprising that stories have changed and become more unforgiving with time, like those from Draper's informants.

225. Wilcox, *House in the Horseshoe*, 239.

226. Conrad, *Papers of Nathanael Greene*, Vol. IX, 233.

227. Gibbes, *Documentary History*, 10.

228. *Orderly Book of General Nathanael Greene*, August 24 entry; Conrad, *Papers of Nathanael Greene*, Vol. IX, 223.

229. Scoggins and Moss, *African American Loyalists*, 39, 88.

230. Newlin, *Battle of Lindley's Mill*, 3. There is disagreement on numbers involved; Caruthers collected stories from both sides.

231. Ibid., 8–9, 12.

232. Caruthers, *Revolutionary Incidents*, 167.

233. Ibid.

234. Dudley, "Sketch of the Military Services." Other reports confirm that some of the worst plunderers in the British army were the females.

235. Dunkerley, *Redcoats on the River*, 233.

236. Rees, "Proportion of Women." A lot of women were with Washington's army that went from New York to Virginia in 1781 to fight at Yorktown.

237. Conrad, *Papers of Nathanael Greene*, Vol. X, 81.

238. Ibid., 443.

239. Ibid., 481.

240. Mayer, *Belonging to the Army*, 143; McCrady, *History of South Carolina*, 614, 621.

241. Mayer, *Belonging to the Army*, 143; McCrady, *History of South Carolina*, 521–22; Johnson, *Life and Correspondence*, 319; Conrad, *Papers of Nathanael Greene*, Vol. X, 81–2.

242. Conrad, *Papers of Nathanael Greene*, Vol. XI, 142.

243. Ibid., 337.

Conclusion

244. Braisted, "Female Ancestors."

245. Wolf, *As Various as Their Land*, 11.

Bibliography

An Account of Articles Received at New Garden Meeting House for the Use of Wounded Prisoners, March 20, 1781. Cornwallis Papers, 30/11/5, 179, Public Records Office, Kew, Surry, England.

Babits, Lawrence. *A Devil of a Whipping.* Chapel Hill: University of North Carolina Press, 1998.

Bass, Robert D. *Ninety Six.* Lexington, SC: Sandlapper, 1978.

The Battle of Huck's Defeat and an Account of the Unveiling of the Monument by the Kings Mountain Chapter, Daughters of the American Revolution. Yorkville, SC, 1895.

Berkin, Carol. *Revolutionary Mothers.* New York: Vintage Books, 2005.

Black, C.J. *History of the First Baptist Church of Kings Mountain, NC.* Kings Mountain, NC: The Herald Publishing House, 1926.

Black, Hugh. Federal Pension Application. R 983. Washington, D.C.: National Archives.

Blumenthal, Walter Hart. *Women Camp Followers of the American Revolution.* New York: Arno Press, 1974.

Booraem, Hendrick. *Young Hickory.* Dallas, TX: Taylor Trade, 2001.

Borick, Carl. *A Gallant Defense.* Columbia: University of South Carolina Press, 2003.

Braisted, Todd. "Female Ancestors, Refugees and Others." www.royalprovincial.com/geneaology/fems/fams4.shtml. Accessed March 26, 2007.

Brown, Katherine M. *Good Wives, Nasty Wenches, and Anxious Patriarchs.* Chapel Hill: University of North Carolina Press, 1996.

Carr, James O., ed. *The Dickson Letters.* Raleigh, NC: Edwards and Broughton, 1901.

Caruthers, Eli. *Revolutionary Incidents and Sketches of Character Chiefly in the Old North State*. Philadelphia: Hayes and Zell, 1854.

Claghorn, Charles. *Women Patriots of the American Revolution*. Metuchen, NJ: Scarecrow Press Inc., 1991.

Clinton, James. Federal Pension Application. S2437. Washington, D.C.: National Archives.

Collins, James. *Autobiography of a Revolutionary Soldier*. North Stratford, NH: Ayer Company Publishers, 2006.

Conrad, Dennis, ed. *The Papers of Nathanael Greene*. Vol. VIII. Chapel Hill: University of North Carolina Press, 1994.

———. *The Papers of Nathanael Greene*. Vol. IX. Chapel Hill: University of North Carolina Press, 1997.

———. *The Papers of Nathanael Greene*. Vol. X. Chapel Hill: University of North Carolina Press, 1998.

———. *The Papers of Nathanael Greene*. Vol. XI. Chapel Hill: University of North Carolina Press, 2000.

Cornwallis, Lord Charles, to Lord Francis Rawdon. February 21, 1781. Cornwallis Papers, 30/11/87, Public Records Office, Kew, Surry, England.

Curtis, Edward E. *The British Army in the American Revolution*. Gansevoort, NY: Corner House Historical Publishing, 1998.

Demond, Robert O. *The Loyalists in North Carolina During the Revolution*. Baltimore: Clearfield Co. Inc., 2002.

DePauw, Linda Grant. "Women in Combat: The Revolutionary War Experience." *Armed Forces and Society* 7 (1981): 209–26.

Draper, Lyman C. Draper Manuscript Collection. Madison, WI: State Historical Society of Wisconsin, 15 DD 44,15 DD 61, 4 DD 102, 13 DD 85, 6 DD 13, 6 DD 143, 6 DD 126, 6 DD 134, 6 DD 153, 6 DD 155, 9 VV 30, 13 VV 144, 13 VV 178-200, 14 VV 177, 14 VV 209, 15 VV 311, 16 VV 47, 16 VV 55, 16 VV 70-71, 23 VV 232–4.

———. *Kings Mountain and Its Heroes*. Johnson City, TN: Overmountain Press, 1996.

Dudley, Guilford. "A Sketch of the Military Services Performed by Guilford Dudley, Then of the Town of Halifax, North Carolina, During the Revolutionary War." *Southern Literary Messenger* (March–June 1845).

Dunkerly, Robert M. *Kings Mountain Walking Tour Guide*. Pittsburgh: Dorrance Publishing, 2003.

———. *Redcoats on the River*. Wilmington, NC: Dram Tree Press, 2008.

Dunkerly, Robert M., and Eric K. Williams. *Old Ninety Six: A History and Guide*. Charleston, SC: The History Press, 2006.

Bibliography

Durham, Robert Lee. "Woman Buried With Ferguson On King's Mountain Says Robert L. Durham; An Interesting Incident." *Cleveland Star*, February 24, 1930.

Ellet, Elizabeth. *The Women of the Revolution*. New York: Baker and Scribner, 1849.

Fagan, Brian. *The Little Ice Age*. New York: Basic Books, 2000.

Fischer, Kristen. *Suspect Relations*. Ithaca, NY: Cornell University Press, 2002.

Frey, Silvia. *Water From the Rock*. Princeton: Princeton University Press, 1991.

Fryar, Jack, ed. *Benson J. Lossing's Pictorial Field-Book of the Revolution in the Carolinas & Georgia*. Wilmington, NC: Dram Tree Books, 2004.

Gibbes, Robert. *Documentary History of the American Revolution*. New York: D. Appleton & Co., 1857.

Gilchrist, Marianne M. *Patrick Ferguson*. Edinburgh, UK: NMS Enterprises Ltd., 1998.

Gordon, James. Federal Pension Application. S2437. Washington, D.C.: National Archives.

Graham, James. *Life of General Daniel Morgan*. New York: Derby and Jackson, 1859.

Greene, Jerome. *Historic Resources Study and Historic Structure Report, Ninety Six: A Historical Narrative*. Denver: National Park Service, 1978.

Gruber, Ira, ed. *John Peeble's The American War*. Mechanicsburg, PA: Stackpole Books, 1998.

Hagist, Don. "The Women of the Army." Revwar75.com/library.hagist/britwomen.htm#127. Accessed March 20, 2007.

Helsley, Alexia Jones. *South Carolinians in the War of American Independence*. Columbia: South Carolina Department of Archives and History.

Howard, Robert A., and E. Alvin Gerhardt Jr. *Mary Patton*. Rocky Mount, TN: Rocky Mount Historical Association, 1980.

Hubbell, S. Michael. *Mystery of Moores Creek*. Report on file in park archives. 1961.

Hubbell, S. Michael, to Charles Hatch. Office Memorandum, 1962. Moores Creek National Battlefield Park archives.

James, Charles, ed. *The Siege of Savannah*. New York: Arno Press, 1968.

Johnson, William. *Sketches of the Life and Correspondence of Nathanael Greene*. New York: Da Capo Press, 1973.

Kennett, Lee. "Killing on Minden Road: Man Fatally Stabbed By Girl With Pitchfork." *Pleasant Garden Post*, November 5, 1999.

Kierner, Cynthia. *Beyond the Household*. Ithaca, NY: Cornell University Press, 1998.

————. *Southern Women in Revolution*. Columbia: University of South Carolina Press, 1998.

Kopperman, Paul E. "The British High Command and Soldier's Wives in America, 1755–1783." *Journal of the Society for Army Historical Research* 60 (Spring 1982): 14–34.

Landrum, J.B.O. *History of Spartanburg County*. Atlanta: Franklin Printing and Publishing Co., 1900.

Latham, Robert. *Revolutionary War in the Upcountry of South Carolina*. Broad River Basin Historical Society, 1998.

Lee, Robert E, ed. *The Revolutionary War Memoirs of General Henry Lee*. New York: Da Capo Press, 1998.

Levins, Sandy. "Was Death by Fire Common in Colonial Kitchens?" http:/historic.camdencounty.com/ccnews21.shtml. Accessed July 28, 2007.

Lossing, Benson. *Reflections of Rebellion*. Charleston, SC: The History Press, 2005.

MacLeod, Ruairidh H. *Flora MacDonald*. London: Shepheard Walwyn Publishers, 1995.

Martin, James K., and Mark E. Lender. *A Respectable Army*. Arlington Heights, IL: Harlan Davidson Inc., 1982.

Mayer, Holly. *Belonging to the Army*. Columbia: University of South Carolina Press, 1996.

Maze, Terry, to Frank Haines. Wilmington, NC, July 14, 1975. Park Archives, Moores Creek National Battlefield, Currie, NC.

McCrady, Edward. *The History of South Carolina in the Revolution*. New York: Russell and Russell, 1969.

McQueen, John. Federal Pension Application. S30577. Washington, D.C.: National Archives.

Moore, Christopher. *The Loyalists*. Toronto: M&S, 1984.

Moss, Bobby. *Loyalists at Ninety Six*. Blacksburg, SC: Scotia Hibernia Press, 1999.

————. *Patriots at Cowpens*. Blacksburg, SC: Scotia Hibernia Press, 1985.

————. *Patriots at Kings Mountain*. Blacksburg, SC: Scotia Hibernia Press, 1990.

————. *Uzal Johnson: Loyalist Surgeon*. Blacksburg, SC: Scotia Hibernia Press, 2000.

Moultrie, William. *Memoirs of the American Revolution*. New York: Arno Press, 1968.

Newlin, Algie. *The Battle of Lindley's Mill*. Burlington, NC: Alamance Historical Association, 1975.

Newsome, A.R., ed. "A British Orderly Book." *North Carolina Historical Review* 9, no. 3 (July 1932): 273–98; no. 4 (October 1932): 366–92.

Norton, Mary Beth. *Liberty's Daughters*. Ithaca, NY: Cornell University Press, 1980.

———. "What An Alarming Crisis This Is: Southern Women and the American Revolution." In *The Southern Experience in the American Revolution*, edited by Jeffrey Crow and Larry Tise, 203–34. Chapel Hill: University of North Carolina, 1978.

Orderly Book of General Nathanael Greene's Southern Campaign From April 5th to September 4th, 1781. Society of the Cincinnati, Washington, D.C.

The Pennsylvania Housewife. Harleysville, PA: Past Masters, 2003.

Rees, John U. "Boiling the Pot Everyday: Soldier's Food and Cooking in the War of Independence." *Brigade of the American Revolution* 30.

———. "The Foundation of an Army is the Belly: North American Soldier's Food 1765–1945." ALHFAM Proceedings of the 1998 Conference and Annual Meeting, vol. 21: 49–64. ALHFAM, Bloomfield, OH.

———. "The Multitude of Women." Revwar75.com/library/rees/ wnumb1.htm. Accessed March 20, 2007.

———. "The Number of Rations Issued to the Women in camp." Revwar75.com/library/rees/. Accessed March 20, 2007.

———. "The Proportion of Women Which Ought to be allowed." Revwar75.com/library/rees/proportion.htm#12. Accessed March 20, 2007.

Robinson, Blackwell P. *A History of Moore County*. Southern Pines, NC: Moore County Historical Society, 1956.

Royal Gazette. New York. October 8, 1780.

Royster, Charles. *A Revolutionary People At War*. Chapel Hill: University of North Carolina Press, 1986.

Salley, Alexander S. *Records of the Regiments of the South Carolina Line in the Revolutionary War*. Baltimore: Clearfield Co., 1977.

Saye, James. *Memoirs of Major Joseph McJunkin*. Spartanburg, SC: A Press Inc., 1847.

Scheer, George, and Hugh Rankin. *Rebels and Redcoats*. New York: Da Capo Press, 1987.

Scoggins, Michael. *The Day it Rained Militia*. Charleston, SC: The History Press, 2005.

Scoggins, Michael, and Bobby Moss. *African American Loyalists in the Southern Campaigns of the American Revolution*. Blacksburg, SC: Scotia Hibernia Press, 2006.

Selsky, Harold E. *A Demographic Survey of the Continental Army That Wintered at Valley Forge, PA, 1777–78*. New Haven, CT, 1987.

Slocumb, Ezekiel. Federal Pension Application. S7526. Washington, D.C.: National Archives.

Smith, Karen A. Unpublished research on clothing in the South Carolina backcountry.

———. "What Really Killed Women in the 18th Century?" *Kings Mountain National Military Park Newsletter*, Summer 2005.

Smith, Steven D., James B. Legg, Tamara S. Wilson and Jonathan Leader. *"Obstinate and Strong": The History and Archaeology of the Siege of Fort Motte*. Columbia: South Carolina Institute of Archaeology and Anthropology, 2007.

Spruill, Julia. *Women's Life and Work in the Southern Colonies*. New York: W.W. Norton, 1977.

Stedman, Charles. *The History of the Origin, Progress, and Termination of the American War*. London, 1794.

Tarleton, Banastre. *A History of the Campaigns of 1780 and 1781 in the Southern Provinces of North America*. North Stratford, NH: Ayer Publishing, 2001.

Thompson, Bill, and Guy Smith. *The Early History of the House in the Horseshoe*. House in the Horseshoe Preservation Committee Inc., 1999.

Travers, Carolyn Freeman. "Were They All Shorter Back Then?" www.plimoth.org/discover/myth/4-ft-2.pnp.

Trussell, John B.B. *The Pennsylvania Line*. Harrisburg: Pennsylvania Historical and Museum Commission, 1993.

Tulley, Mark. *The Packet*. Baraboo, WI: Ballindalloch Press, 1999.

———. *The Packet II*. Baraboo, WI: Ballindalloch Press, 2000.

———. *The Packet IV*. Baraboo, WI: Ballindalloch Press, 2006.

Tustin, Joseph P., ed and trans. *Diary of the American War*. New Haven, CT: Yale University Press, 1979.

Wallace, John. Federal Pension Application. W955. Washington, D.C.: National Archives.

Ward, Christopher. *The War of the Revolution*. Vol. 2. New York: McMillan Co., 1952.

Watson, Alan D. "Women in Colonial North America: Overlooked and Underestimated." *North Carolina Historical Review* 58 (1981): 1–22.

Wellman, Manly W. *The Story of Moore County*. Moore County Historical Society, 1974.

Wickwire, Franklin, and Mary Wickwire. *Cornwallis: The American Adventure*. Boston: Houghton Mifflin Co., 1970.

Wilcox, George. *A History of the House in the Horseshoe*. Wilmington, NC: Historical Resource Services, 1999.

Wilkinson, Eliza. *Letters of Eliza Wilkinson*. New York: Arno Press, 1969.

Wilson, David K. *The Southern Strategy*. Charleston: University of South Carolina Press, 2005.

Wolf, Stephanie G. *As Various as Their Land*. New York: HarperCollins, 1993.

Wright, John Womack. *Some Notes on the Continental Army*. Vails Gate, NY: National Temple Hill Association, 1975.

Young, Marjorie. *South Carolina Women Patriots of the American Revolution*. Anderson: South Carolina Landmark Conference, 1979.

Zachman, Jon. E-mail to author, February 3, 2007.

About the Author

Robert M. Dunkerly is currently chief ranger of Moores Creek National Battlefield near Wilmington, North Carolina. He holds a degree in history from St. Vincent College and a master's degree in historic preservation from Middle Tennessee State University. He has worked at eight historic sites, and written several books and articles on the Revolution, Civil War and historical commemoration. He is active in historic preservation, and has visited over three hundred battlefields worldwide. He and his fiancée Karen live within the 1781 British defenses in downtown Wilmington.

Please visit us at

www.historypress.net